Quality Imperatives in Long-Term Care:
The Elusive Agenda

Quality Imperatives in Long-Term Care:
The Elusive Agenda

Ethel L. Mitty, Editor

National League for Nursing Press • New York
Pub. No. 41-2440

ISBN 0-88737-536-7

This book was set in Goudy by Publications Development Company.
The editor and designer was Rachel Schaperow. Automated
Graphic Systems was the printer and binder. The cover was
designed by Lillian Welsh.

Printed in the United States of America

Contents

Contributors

Phillip Boyle, PhD, is Associate for Ethical Studies, The Hastings Center, Briarcliff, New York.

Bart Collopy, PhD, is Associate for Ethical Studies, Third Age Center, Fordham University, New York, New York.

Sister Rosemary Donley, PhD, RN, FAAN, is Executive Vice President, The Catholic University of America, Washington, D.C., and Former President, National League for Nursing.

Marsha Fretwell, MD, is Head, Program in Geriatric Medicine, Brown University, Roger Williams General Hospital, Department of Medicine, Providence, Rhode Island.

Robert B. Friedland is Director of Public Policy, Project Hope, Washington, D.C.

Sheldon L. Goldberg is President, American Association of Homes for the Aging, Washington, D.C.

Bruce Jennings is Executive Director of The Hastings Center, Briarcliff, New York.

Pamela J. Maraldo, PhD, RN, FAAN, is Chief Executive Officer, National League for Nursing, New York, New York.

Maria Mitchell, MS, CPNP, RN, is Senior Vice President, Community Health Accreditation Program, National League for Nursing, New York, New York.

Ethel L. Mitty, EdD, RN, is Assistant Administrator, Nursing Services, North Shore University Hospital Center for Extended Care and Rehabilitation, Manhasset, New York.

Mary Ousley, RN, is Executive Director, Provider Management Development, Richmond, Kentucky.

Paul R. Wilging, PhD, is Executive Vice President, American Health Care Association, Washington, D.C.

Introduction

Quality of care (and of life) is the primary issue in institutional long-term care. It is inseparable from the issues of cost (i.e., resource use) and, more recently, of ethics. Public policy determinations to assure quality are realized through legislation and regulations despite the paucity of reliable indicators of quality. Indeed, the very definition of quality remains elusive; we have strong feelings about "it," we make reference to "it," we quantify the absence of "it." The Eighth National League for Nursing Invitational Long-Term Conference brought together experts and leaders from education, service, and provider associations to continue the discussion of assuring quality in long-term care. From a historical perspective, this conference was particularly timely in view of the recent enactment of a major piece of federal legislation designed to assure quality in long-term care: OBRA 1987.

Held annually with the generous assistance of Ross Laboratories, and following program themes developed by the Long-Term Care Committee of the NLN, the first five-year series of conferences, 1982–1987, was based on the theme, "Overcoming the bias of ageism through education, research, and evaluation." One of the topics covered during this five-year period dealt with the shortage of nurses in long-term care, "Attracting nurses through optional educational experiences." Other topics included "Models for continuity of care," "Community-based initiatives—creative change," and "Educational models."

This volume presents the proceedings of the third invitational conference within the second five-year series, 1989–1993. The overall theme for this series is "Quality in the Long-Term Care Marketplace:

Indices, Costs, Mechanisms, Ethics, Public Policy." Each conference is required to consider cost and ethics within the context of the topic. In 1989, the topic was "Indices of Quality: Research." Developments in research pertinent to quality of care in long-term care were presented from the perspective of education, practice, and the client. One outcome of this meeting was the development of a Delphi study to set the research agenda for long-term care in the 1990s. In 1990, the topic was "Mechanisms of Quality: Service." Papers from this conference described quality assurance activities in institutional and community practice settings and focused on community expectations and regulatory initiatives to assure quality. The proceedings of these conferences have been published in separate editions.

The 1991 conference, *Quality Imperatives in Long-Term Care: The Elusive Agenda,* brought together individuals from the public and private sectors to discuss recent federal policy relating to quality concerns in the long-term care "marketplace." Topics included an overview of quality imperatives, future directions for the provider, OBRA as a measure of quality, economic and political trends, and private sector initiatives to achieve quality and accreditation. Future invitational conferences are "Mechanisms of Quality: Education" (1992) and "Integration of Research and Education for Quality Long-Term Care" (1993). The expansion of the need for long-term care, both institutional and community-based, challenges providers, consumers, and policy-makers from a variety of perspectives, that is, access, appropriateness, staffing, education, resource use, ethics, cost, and quality. The publication of this volume speaks to the commitment of the NLN to foster communication with long-term care associations, nursing interest-groups (i.e., practice, education, research, administration), and concerned business and consumer groups for the purposes of assuring quality in long-term care through networking and consensus building.

QUALITY IMPERATIVES IN LONG-TERM CARE: THE ELUSIVE AGENDA—AN OVERVIEW

Reiterated throughout the conference was the recognition that no definition of quality would be complete without reference to patient autonomy (note: By OBRA regulation, the "patient" in a nursing facility—no longer called a "nursing home"—is to be called a "resident"). Indeed, the word *empowerment* is as applicable, and important, to the resident as it is to the nurse in a "shared governance" institutional setting. Several important points were made: (1) that the resident is not divorced from community mores and norms; (2) that the resident's biological/medical needs are not necessarily the most important "quality" issues; (3) that the "customer's" value system had to be incorporated into the plan of care *and* the indices of quality; (4) that survey and regulations for quality assurance should move away from "retrospective-punitive" to "prospective-educational"; and (5) that the notion of quality contained elements of justice, fairness, and faithfulness.

Fretwell used the hologram synthesis to suggest that the seeds of quality assurance are contained in the whole even though we see only one view at a time. Her concept of *continuous quality improvement* (CQI), based on the notion of "shared responsibility," asks us to reject "dualistic thinking" as a way of assigning blame *and* correction of negative quality outcomes. This first paper set the tone for thinking about quality as a joint venture between caregiver and care receiver, between provider and payer, between education and practice and research. The fact that aging people age differently from each other is a point that we may need to state over and over before we determine the boundaries of acceptable quality of care.

Sr. Donley suggested that the *lack of agreement about the nature of health itself* might be a less than conspicuous issue with respect to establishing indices of quality. She noted that if we intend to follow through on OBRA's requirement that resident and family be involved with decisions about care, then meaningful discussion about the quality of care had to recognize that "health is a peculiarly personal reality." Sr. Donley's discussion of the notion of justice as a concomitant of quality of life is especially helpful.

Wilging characterizes OBRA 1987 as a "watershed" piece of long-term care legislation and regulation. His discussion of *highest practicable level of physical and mental well-being*, in an environment that strongly fosters residents' rights, the core of OBRA, is particularly enlightening historically, financially, and operationally. He points out that while staff attitude and motivation are necessary for quality outcomes, they are not sufficient. Training and resources are also needed.

Ousley, a "reactor" to Wilging's paper, reflects that what is contained in OBRA has been standard practice in nursing facilities for many years. Is OBRA an indicator of quality? A measure of quality? She proposed the concept of "positive harm vs. negative harm" wherein the former is a "failure to achieve" and the latter is a "negative outcome of care." Emphasizing that the "highest practicable" measure is the most significant aspect of OBRA, Ousley explains that one "measure" of this is that the resident is not to deteriorate unless it is clearly shown (documented) that this was unavoidable. She reviews the purpose of the resident assessment instrument in its relation to care planning and outcomes.

Goldberg states that one of the most important sources of information with respect to quality of care will come from the residents themselves. In support of previous speakers and summarizing discussion thus far, he points to the provider's dilemma in wanting to provide quality care but being underfunded to do so. Among the issues and opportunities reviewed by Goldberg are: pre-payment and managed-care systems, total quality management (TQM), accreditation, professionalism, and ethics.

Friedland suggests that Medicaid might have been an afterthought to Medicare appropriations. What to do with the elderly needing institutional care? The history of nursing home care, funding, quality, and regulations might have been different had there been adequate planning *and* definition of the setting. Private insurance coverage for institutional and home care is reviewed in "dialogue" with Wilging's earlier comments.

Maraldo draws upon the Skinner behavioral box as analogy for the current lock-step response of the long-term care industry to each regulatory stimulus. Even OBRA is piecemeal and lacks the vision required to move the nursing home industry forward on a national health agenda for quality of care. She draws our attention to seminal issues in health care: the overreliance on high-tech medical care; the imperfect fit of the acute care medical model for long-term care; and the lack of a philosophical understanding, commitment, and description of expectations of nursing home care. Maraldo suggests that bold new approaches are needed to define and assure quality.

Mitchell presents the concept, and describes the operation of, a private sector approach to accreditation of home health agencies, that is,

CHAP. She is particularly committed to the interactive and supportive nature of the CHAP process such that the visitors and "visited" are mutually enthused and involved in striving for, achieving, and maintaining quality. Mitchell describes the role of the client/consumer as a partner in the search for quality indicators. This chapter is unique as well as exciting in that it suggests that there are other ways to "live with regulations"—indeed, to go beyond them—in a way that is meaningful, fun, and speaks to the ethics of a professional group and industry that wants and needs to shake off negative public perceptions.

Mitty had the luxury of reflecting on the entire conference proceedings as well as "reacting" to Mitchell's paper. One clear direction seemed to be an "imperative" to think about quality as a component of education and growth. This has the effect of linking the quality imperatives of OBRA to educational imperatives (for resident/family/consumer and health professional caregiver). She suggests that the concept of *negotiated consent* might be applicable to the quality-of-care survey and the meaningfulness of same. Mitty also looks at the relationship of CQI to principles of adult learning. Some joint research initiatives between the public and private sector are recommended.

The article located in the Appendix was published just a few weeks before the NLN-Ross Invitational Conference; it was mentioned by several of the conference participants. The article, "New Directions in Nursing Home Ethics," by Collopy, Boyle, and Jennings seemed to crystallize the "elusiveness" of quality imperatives in long-term care by focusing on the ambiguity of what nursing home care—and quality—is supposed to be. A product of the Nursing Home Ethics project of The Hastings Center, the "report" covers a broad range of independent yet interrelated issues such as the cultural image of nursing homes, access and placement, institutional constraints and autonomy within community, moral ecology and the paradox of regulation. Several of us planned to use the article as a springboard for discussion within our own institutions and, at the time of publication of this volume, have done so with some interesting results. Probably the most notable and gratifying outcome is that all kinds of staff— from secretaries to caregivers—had never thought about nursing homes and the people who live in them in quite the way the authors described. The article offers us another way of "knowing"; it is highly recommended.

CONCLUSION

The time for eloquence and bombast with respect to quality of long-term care must be put to rest. We need a definition of what long-term care is expected to do, to provide. And we need that commitment supported by appropriate policies, programs, funding, and standards which are not the lowest common denominator, as Goldberg put it, but the highest standard to which everyone can aspire. There was, of course, no final last word about quality at this conference—and rightfully so. The feeling that quality was a perpetually evolving phenomenon, constantly redefining itself as we gain knowledge, skills, and insights, seemed intellectually, holographically, innovatively, and ethically correct.

Ethel L. Mitty, EdD, RN
Assistant Administrator
Nursing Services
North Shore University Hospital Center
    for Extended Care and Rehabilitation
Manhasset, New York

Quality Imperatives in Long-Term Care:
The Elusive Agenda

Quality Imperatives in Long-Term Care

Marsha Fretwell

There have been two major changes in the delivery of long-term care services: (1) the shift in the types of illnesses experienced by patients and (2) the accompanying shift in the care provided by the health professional from palliative to curative to management of chronic disorders. These shifts have created two sets of heretofore unanticipated demands. The first requirement calls for increased responsibility and involvement on the part of the recipient of care in the provision of pertinent information and participation in decision making about his or her plan of care. The second requirement calls for the multiple health professionals involved in providing the care to share the responsibility for the care because no one professional "owns" the patient.

The theory of *continuous improvement in quality systems* provides the opportunity for the sharing of responsibility among the health professionals and the recipient of care so that the goals of an episode of care can be identified, operationalized, assessed, and met. The questions, therefore, are who are the team members, the constituents (patients, clinicians, and administrators), and what are their primary responsibilities as they work together to achieve the goals identified? More than simply process issues, these issues of joint responsibility have an impact on optimal function, accurate diagnoses, appropriate treatment, accurate prognosis, and fiscal solvency. In conceptualizing the responsibilities of each member of this *team*—not traditionally thought of as including the patient—outcome measures for each constituent that will allow him or her to self-monitor his or her own effort must be determined at the outset.

The major barrier to the continuous improvement of quality in long-term care is the "either-or" perception which pervades the very fabric of our culture. Dualistic thinking with respect to the distribution of responsibility, power, control, and information is present within the core structures of our society, family, schools, government, and health care institutions. Either-or thinking may be highly practical for problem-solving but it is highly dysfunctional with respect to identifying quality imperatives in a resource-driven health care delivery system. This type of thinking in health care institutions leads to denial becoming the major coping strategy, fear and greed becoming the major incentives in modifying behavior of the team members, and "crisis intervention" becoming the management style of necessity.

I suggest that a *holographic perspective* may be useful in thinking about quality imperatives for long-term care. Each piece of a hologram contains the entire structure of the hologram. Each piece is not just part of the whole, it contains the entire pattern and way of functioning of the whole embedded in it. As a physician thinking about issues of quality and policy, I feel that I need the firm anchor of what I understand about frail, older patients in order to understand these abstract concepts. If we can come to understand how to achieve one good outcome for one patient, then somewhere in that process we will find the elements of how to understand (and redesign) the entire quality outcomes system. The notion of the hologram can help us see the part as a representation of the whole. Continuous quality improvement systems can be a hologram for learning.

If we apply what we know about the biology of aging, we can arrive at a more rational understanding of quality outcomes or imperatives. The biology of aging can be reduced to two fundamental principles. One is that as we age we have a reduced capacity to deal with stress. We have more difficulty maintaining homeostasis in the face of physical, emotional, or social alterations. Understanding this first principle, we have cause to be quite optimistic about aging because, in fact, despite this profound reduction in the capacity to deal with stress, most older people have a marked capacity to adapt to constant change and remain in balance. The second principle is that as people age, they become more different from each other. The result of this growing uniqueness is that it becomes increasingly difficult to make generalizations about what is right for one person versus what is right for another.

These two principles should inform what a system that is going to provide "good care" for older people should look like. Such a system should not be stressful. It should not add to the problem of maintaining balance. It should address not only physical and medical needs but social and psychological perspectives such that it respects the individual's nature. A seeming paradox is the issue of the preservation of the patient's autonomy in the face of dependency. If we can put aside our dualistic thinking (i.e., that a person is either autonomous or dependent), then we can accept, and indeed be creative about, autonomy within dependency. In thinking about learning and education, one theory holds that we learn from our mistakes. When preparing a diagnostic and therapeutic plan of care, the good practitioner will define the (health) problem in terms of the value system of the patient. Practitioner and patient form a relationship, set goals, and try to reach them. In other words, does the patient "get better"? Do people get better? The process, then, is to set goals, see whether they are achieved, analyze them if they were not, and re-examine our assumptions. This is the process of continuous quality improvement; it avoids fixed, immutable endpoints; it allows us to adapt. It not only is not stressful, it can be fun.

Continuous quality improvement systems encourage capture of the complexities of the individual as well as allow us to constantly readjust assumptions and expectations. The system also readjusts the way we view "blame" and responsibility. A cornerstone of continuous quality improvement is that filtering through the system are the values and preferences of the patient/customer. The issue of the patient/ customer value system is rarely mentioned in the quality-of-care outcomes discussions. An argument can be made that the patient is not the only customer in the quality-of-care system. In institutional long-term care, the patient (now called a resident) is one customer among several. The nursing staff, one could argue, represents another customer within the facility who must be listened to in terms of the process.

If we want to design a quality-of-outcomes system that incorporates residents' demands and the characteristics or processes of care, and one that includes a commitment to learning, then we must shift to a mode of operation which focuses on the prevention of error—a key aspect of continuous quality improvement systems. This last aspect is important because it has a significant relationship to the cost issue. It has been my experience in working with patients and doctors that they do not really expect health care professionals to be perfect. What they expect us to do is to listen to them, incorporate their value system into the care plan, be honest if we do not understand what is going on, and be ready to say "I've got to look it up, I've got to talk to another doctor, I've got to get a second opinion. . . ." It is my conviction that if we constantly work in this mode, we will prevent error *and* we will reduce costs of care.

Another point in support of the continuous quality improvement system is that it fosters shared responsibility. This idea relates back to my earlier point of avoiding either-or situations (i.e., no one professional group "owns" the patient). If we are going to share responsibility, then we must also share information. This means that everyone shares in the process of improving quality. The constituents of the team—patient, clinician, administrator—will each decide what he or she is responsible for, how their respective goals will be met, and what kind of outcome measures are needed to allow self-evaluation.

Why has this seemingly reasonable, rational process not been fully operationalized? While this process has been described in the literature for 40 years, I attribute its slow dissemination to our either-or way of perceiving the world. Stuck in dualistic thought, we say that either "A" is responsible for the problem or "B" is responsible for the problem; responsibility for the problem cannot be shared. It would be patently unfair for the long-term care system to solve a problem which is embedded in society, but we must at least be aware of such problems in order to meet our quality outcomes imperatives.

If the mission of long-term care facilities is to optimize the physical, emotional, and social function of the residents, then the organization of the work must support the mission itself. Returning to the holographic perspective, we need to understand that each aide, each nurse, each physician, each family member, each dietitian—in short, each person working in the facility—operationalizes the mission through his or her work. We need to collect information and feed it back to the members of the team. We must accept change as the norm—just as do our patients. We must keep moving and learning. My perception of the continuous quality improvement system is that it protects us from locked-in solutions or endpoints. It is an appropriate mechanism to initiate and sustain the required changes as we continuously improve the quality of care.

2

Response to "Quality Imperatives in Long-Term Care"

Sister Rosemary Donley

I wish to preface my response to Marsha Fretwell's presentation with a story about an older woman. I present this story as a way of saying that my concern for quality care for older people is more than a professional concern.

I am living with a 95-year-old woman. Some days she has trouble with what her daughter and I call "the television people," the actors and program participants who come into our living room via the television set. Sometimes she thinks they talk to her. One evening several weeks ago, she was very disturbed. She was looking out the window when I arrived home. It seemed to her as if the house were empty. When I entered the kitchen she said, "Will you eat your dinner with me in the living room?" She then pointed to the television set and asked "Can we turn that off?" She began to say something that was very confused and hard for me to interpret. Later, I surmised that she had watched a game show earlier in the day. One of "the television people" had said to her, "you have won $1,000 and a trip to California." Fair enough. Except this happened around income tax time. She thought that the Internal Revenue Service knew that she had won $1,000. She believed they would be coming to visit her that day. She had waited for the IRS all day. One of the Sisters kept saying to her, "No, there are the same number of cars there. There are no new cars in our driveway." The older woman was convinced, however, that the IRS would be coming at any minute.

Matters were worse for her because she did not want to go to California. She wondered whatever prompted those people, whom she did not know, to invite her to California. "What kind of woman do they think I am? Don't they know that I am recovering from pneumonia?" By eleven o'clock, when I had sorted out the events of her day, I said, "I have to make a comment on our society. People today work from nine to five. The IRS people have gone home. They've had their supper; they are getting ready for bed. And you know what? I think you and I should do that too." She looked at me and we went upstairs. She went to bed and has not mentioned this episode again.

I thought about that evening as I reflected upon this conference. I wonder what separates me from her? Is it that I do not think that I will ever win $1,000? Is it that I am not preoccupied with money or my economic future? Are my days less confusing because I have the ability to recognize and tune out conversations that are not directed to me? I am concerned, however, about the effect of the "television people" on the quality of her life and ours.

This meeting was convened to discuss quality of care in long-term care facilities and its continuous improvement. One of the great difficulties we face is in defining what constitutes quality. It seems easier to define quality in terms of what it is *not* than of what it is. For example, we know when we have failed to provide quality education, but we do not know precisely how to define quality education. Have we provided quality education if the students can read or if they can do math or if they move up to the next class? Defining quality of health care is no less difficult. Some federal regulations define quality of care in terms of the presence or absence of indices associated with mortality or morbidity. Other regulations, such as the 1987 Medicare regulations, state that determining whether residents are being restrained is an important indicator of quality care.

I think that part of the difficulty with establishing agreement about positive indices of quality comes from a lack of agreement about the nature of health itself. Discussions about quality care situations, or those processes which seek to improve systematically the quality of care, require a dialogue about the meaning of health and well-being. Linking the sharing of ideas about health and quality does not simplify the dialogue. We need to recognize that health is a peculiarly personal reality. If we wish to engage residents and their families in meaningful discussion about the quality of care, we need to hear and integrate their values about health. If we accept Fretwell's principles that older people tolerate stress less well and are more different than alike, we are compelled to seek a common understanding about the values that the residents and their families associate with health and well-being.

What is the residents' understanding of an optimal state of physical, cognitive, emotional, and social well-being? How does a system of care nourish the development of the processes which lead to these ends? The definitions which flow from these dialogues may not resemble the texts learned in medical and nursing schools. They may, however, help providers accept the life trajectories of their residents and help them understand why some residents can face disability and death with such heroism and others do so with such difficulty.

One valuable aspect of the Fretwell paper is her suggestion of how quality of care might be defined in a more positive manner, to optimize the physical, cognitive, emotional, and social functions of each resident. She amplified this definition with the suggestion that quality care could be better understood and realized if the various caregivers talked to each other about how to achieve continuous quality improvement. Fretwell noted that traditional boundaries and relationships are barriers to professional dialogue and continuous quality improvement. This observation, about the critical importance of professional communication, has been validated in acute-care settings. Findings from the so-called APACHE studies show that patients in intensive-care settings achieve positive, measurable outcomes when physicians and nurses talk to each other about the patients' plans of care (Knaus, Draper, Wagner, & Zimmerman, 1986).

Another important factor in Fretwell's paper is a belief that health providers and residents must be willing to learn from their mistakes. Self-correction requires a level of trust, a sense of autonomy, and a willingness to accept responsibility for error. It also requires an openness to change. The APACHE study reported another significant finding: care outcomes improved when intensive-care nurses continued their education (Knaus et al., 1986). I believe education creates a climate that is conducive to change and learning from one's mistakes.

What would an optimal care environment look like? It would be characterized by a willingness to share the burdens of each other (staff and residents) so that disability, disorientation, denial, or error would not alienate a person from him or herself or from the group. It would play to the strengths of the persons in the environment, not their weaknesses. It would seek to minimize personal and professional stress. A caring environment would use color, light, and texture to enhance human enjoyment and orientation. Caring environments would be welcoming and make a person feel at home. Dialogue and communication would be the currency of an environment which seeks to optimize physical, cognitive, emotional, and social well-being. Persons would listen and seek to understand the experience as well as the speech and behavior of the other. Professionals would be more motivated by the common goal of an enhanced caring environment than by the need to maintain the status quo and hierarchical structures of control.

Justice and the related notions of autonomy and dignity are being given increasing attention in the health care literature (Daniel, 1988). Concern for justice and the integrity of human relationships is a prerequisite for quality of care. In contemporary ethical literature, the notion of justice is spelled out: justice is equality of participation or equality of opportunity. This notion of justice requires that each person be able to participate, in his or her significant relationships, to the fullest extent possible (Daniel, 1985; Kapp, 1989; "Economic Justice," 1986). Application of the concept of justice as participation would require that persons in long-term care environments be helped to maintain the highest degree of intellectual and personal integrity of which they are capable.

One question which does not seem to be adequately addressed in the discussion of continuous improvement of quality is the question of motivation—why would someone want to assist the dependent elderly to achieve or maintain their highest level of functioning. In the tradition in which I have been raised, religion provides the necessary inspiration. The Hebrew scripture and the Christian testament express an understanding of the biblical sense of justice as fidelity to relationships. Nursing homes can teach us about fidelity to personal and professional relationships. We have observed faithfulness to a frail wife or an aged mother. We have been the caregivers who maintain the integrity and dignity of persons who lose their ability to speak or to choose. An environment which optimizes well-being is an environment supportive of dignity and integrity. It provides for residents who are able to represent themselves as it supports those individuals who depend totally, for their life and well-being, upon their caregivers and the environment.

Professional employees in acute-care institutions are influenced by many structures of power, not the least of which are their placement and autonomy in the parent organization. The values operative in clinical units come from many sources: professional ethics, specialty training, expectations of hospital (employers and medical staff), various licensing and accrediting boards, and professional practice acts. In one sense, it is naive to think that a group of institutionally employed professionals, working under the aegis of a department of nursing and an interdisciplinary team, can transcend the environment of the institution where practice acts, institutional policies, and medical directives regulate clinical responsibilities. Relevant to the discussion is the nursing literature on autonomy which describes the gap between the clinical authority of nurses and their responsibility for patient care (Prescott & Dennis, 1985). Hospital nurses have allegiance to patients, families, coworkers, organizational superiors, physicians, and codes of professional practice. While the ordering of these values varies with the nurse and the situation, most nurses report a tension between their responsibility for care and their lack of autonomy for clinical decision making (Prescott & Dennis, 1985). Interdisciplinary team members need to share authority and responsibility. Given the controlling nature of bureaucracies, radical change in the mode of clinical governance can more easily be accomplished at the institutional or macro level than at the unit level. The purpose of this digression is to highlight the significant role of governing and influencing structures on care environments.

Fretwell believes that care environments can be enhanced if professionals and residents share responsibility for care. I think that the long-term care delivery system requires a radical reform of the power structures which influence clinical decision making. Fretwell proposes that the functioning of residents will be optimized along a continuum of cognitive, physical, emotional, and social well-being if professionals and residents engage in a process of continuous quality improvement and learn from their mistakes. I think that the improvement of the well-being of residents requires a clearer articulation of the operative values about health and quality of long-term care. More significantly, I believe that the motivation to engage in quality enhancement requires a deeper commitment than is provided by the regulatory environment of OBRA (Omnibus Budget Reconciliation Act of 1987) or the adoption of a method of quality improvement. Such motivation requires a belief in the fundamental dignity of the person and an espousal of a professional mode of practice characterized by a concern for justice and fidelity to human relationships.

REFERENCES

Daniel, N. (1985). *Just health care*. Cambridge: Cambridge University Press.

Daniel, N. (1988). *Am I my brother's keeper*. New York: Oxford University Press.

Economic Justice for All, Pastoral Letter on Catholic Social Teaching and the U.S. Economy (1986). Washington, D.C.: National Conference of Catholic Bishops.

Kapp, M. B. (1989). Medical empowerment of the elderly. *Hastings Center Report, 19*, 5–7.

Knaus, W., Draper, E., Wagner, D., & Zimmerman, J. (1986). An evaluation of outcome from intensive care in major medical centers. *Annals of Internal Medicine, 104*, 410–418.

Prescott, P., & Dennis, K. (1985). Power and powerlessness in hospital nursing departments. *Journal of Professional Nursing, 1*,(6), 348–355.

Veatch, R. (1981). *A theory of medical ethics*. New York: Basic Books.

3

A Strategy for Quality Assurance in Long-Term Care

Paul R. Wilging

Quality of nursing home care has proven to be one of the most politically volatile—yet societally critical—issues confronting the American public. The issue strikes at the core of individual concern about possible functional impairment and potential loss of independence. Complicated by the likelihood of personal impoverishment, long-term care issues become even more problematic and worthy of understanding, analysis, and action.

Issues relating to quality must be viewed within the context of available financial and human resources. With regard to payment, Medicare is a relatively minor player, having paid only 5 percent of the total nursing home bill in 1990. However, an understanding of the flaws inherent in the current payment mechanism is essential to an awareness of the dynamics of long-term care for two reasons.

First, Medicaid, the federal-state poverty program, pays nearly one-half of all nursing home costs. Without question, the severely inadequate Medicaid reimbursement rates in many states have a direct bearing on the quality of care available to Medicare beneficiaries, since a facility's ability to provide quality services to all patients is directly affected by the adequacy of revenue available to pay for services.

In addition, current Medicaid payment rates, as low as $40 per day in many states, make recruitment and retention of nursing personnel difficult, at best. Certainly, the etiology of the current nurse shortage is complex, but one factor must be addressed if nursing homes are to find workable solutions: nurse salaries must be increased. This issue is not easily remedied because state-imposed Medicaid rates determine the parameters within which nursing home salaries are set.

Complicating the problem is the fact that the Omnibus Budget Reconciliation Act of 1987 has imposed new nurse staffing requirements on nursing homes at a time when enrollment in nursing schools is falling, competition for already scarce nursing personnel is increasing, and high paying nurse registries are drawing potential employees away from long-term care practice.

It is only with an understanding of these two critical issues that a realistic discussion of quality assurance activities in nursing homes can take place.

QUALITY CARE IN NURSING HOMES

If we understand quality of care to be the delivery of health care services in such a fashion as to most efficiently, effectively, and humanely return the patient to—or maintain the patient at—his or her highest level of functioning, then programs which fail to do so cannot be deemed to be meeting quality standards. With respect to nursing home care in the United States, it is the structural and financial flaws in the Medicare and Medicaid programs themselves which most impede the provision of high quality care.

Too often the approach to quality of care in nursing homes has focused exclusively on regulation. Attention has not been focused on the fiscal and programmatic environment within which providers are forced to operate. A two-and-one-half-year study released by the Institute of Medicine in 1986 is a case in point.

Entitled *Improving the Quality of Care in Nursing Homes*, the study contained more than 400 pages of analysis and recommendations focusing on nursing home regulatory changes. While the study's recommendations were sound, and supported by long-term care providers nationally, quality problems were viewed primarily as a function of provider attitudes and skills.

There is no question that attitudes and skills relate directly to the level of quality provided in a nursing home. For that reason, the American Health Care Association (AHCA) joined with the National Citizens' Coalition for Nursing Home Reform and several other provider and consumer organizations to urge Congress to develop legislation implementing many of the Institute of Medicine's recommendations. Passed in 1987 as part of OBRA, the law included new regulatory requirements in several areas, among them the following:

- Development of an in-depth, uniform resident assessment tool;
- Improved tools for measuring the quality of patient care—with a focus on patient outcome rather than paperwork requirements;
- Improved training for surveyors;
- Increased nurse staffing requirements;
- Elimination of the distinction between skilled nursing facilities and intermediate care facilities;
- Nurse aide training requirements; and
- Additional enforcement mechanisms.

With regulations currently being drafted to implement OBRA provisions—and with nursing facilities already implementing the law—most experts agree that the regulatory mechanism is in place for assuring the highest quality of care in the nation's nursing homes.

A strong argument could be made, however, that it is precisely the preoccupation with the regulatory determinants of quality that has created the greatest difficulty in assuring quality. For more than 20 years, questions about quality have been answered with more layers of regulation: new criteria for care, new systems of review, more surveyors and quality assurance specialists.

Yet, few would argue that the quality of care—and the quality of life—offered to America's nursing home patients is largely a function of resource availability, both in terms of staff and dollars.

QUALITY: THE NEED FOR
ADEQUATE RESOURCES

As providers, consumers, and policymakers look forward to ensuring the availability of high quality long-term care services to a growing number of aging Americans, they must address two key issues:

- How do we design a financing system that is humane and digni-fied, while providing sufficient funding to assure that all nurs-ing home providers can deliver the highest quality of care possible?
- To what extent can federal policies help alleviate the current shortage of nurses—especially in long-term care nursing—which clearly affects the level of quality available to all nursing home residents?

The AHCA feels that in the long run, a complete revamping of the current financing system is essential to assure that quality long-term care will be available to all Americans who need it. Given the constraints of the current federal budget deficit, AHCA supports a fiscally responsible approach, which relies on the private sector to play a more dominant role. The expansion of private insurance for long-term care—and the development of adequate consumer protections as well as reasonable premiums and benefits—is essential. As a result of an expanded private sector role, the quality of long-term care services would no longer be determined by state Medicaid officials trying to control tightening budgets.

The availability of nurses is another problem that affects the level of quality in nursing homes. In the short run, policymakers must work with consumers and providers to find solutions to the nurse shortage, a problem that in nursing homes has been exacerbated by the failings of the current Medicaid-based payment system. If quality of care is to be assured, nursing homes must be able to compete with other health care providers for skilled staff to care for the increasingly dependent nursing home population.

Salary data provide some insight into the problem. Registered nurses earn an average of 35 percent less in nursing homes than in hospitals. More specifically, registered nurses working as administrators earn 49 percent less, supervisors earn 34 percent less, head nurses earn 31 percent less, and staff nurses earn 23 percent less than their hospital counterparts. Similar salary differentials are found in comparing other nursing personnel employed in nursing homes and hospitals.

Therefore, AHCA promotes a short-term approach to dealing with the nurse shortage, which requires Medicaid program changes to provide a wage pass-through for nurse salaries. Action on this issue will allow nursing homes participating in federal programs to offer competitive wages that reflect staff skills and knowledge.

In the long term, however, we must develop strategic approaches to ensuring the availability of all levels of licensed nursing staff. The projected growth in the number of elderly will have a profound impact on where nursing personnel will be needed and used in the next decade. In fact, dramatic shifts will take place in the relative need for more registered and licensed practical nurses in both the nursing home and hospital industries. While hospitals are expected to need an increase of 10 percent of registered nurses and fewer licensed practical nurses by the year 2,000, nursing homes are expected to need 125 percent more registered nurses and 142 percent more practical nurses. If nursing home patients are sicker and need a greater level of intensity of care—a trend which is already under way—the need for even greater numbers of nurses in the long-term care setting is likely.

Because of the projected need, a much greater emphasis must be placed on educating geriatric nurses and providing the necessary incentives to facilitate their working in long-term care settings.

DEVELOPING EFFECTIVE TECHNICAL QUALITY ASSESSMENT TOOLS

Clearly, in implementing OBRA, policymakers dealt with the first half of the quality equation in nursing homes by developing the appropriate regulatory environment within which facilities must operate. The second part of the equation is yet to be solved: ensuring that the necessary resources are available to provide a high quality of care and a high quality of life for all nursing home patients.

As the second part of the equation is being debated, policymakers must also work toward developing a useful and accurate tool for measuring quality. It is important to understand that the difficulty encountered in trying to review and assess the level of quality offered in nursing homes is rooted in the fact that nursing homes provide not only medical and nursing services to their patients, they also provide the social services and activity programs necessary in long-term care. The nursing home is not simply a medical care facility, it is also a home. In a home setting, the quality of a patient's life becomes a key determinant of quality care.

To properly measure the quality of care provided in nursing homes, therefore, it is essential that meaningful and measurable definitions of quality of care and quality of life be developed. Such definitions must be tied to patient characteristics and patient needs. This is especially true with regard to nursing home care since in recent years nursing home patients' acuity levels have steadily increased, due in large part to the implementation of the Medicare-based hospital reimbursement system.

Certainly, a refinement of current quality assessment tools must continue. To be reliable indicators of quality, such tools must be patient oriented and outcome based. They must be consistent and positive in their measurement of quality—not simply indicators of technical procedures not followed.

Perhaps the most significant progress made with regard to developing a reliable quality assessment tool came with the passage of OBRA in 1987. In that legislation, Congress mandated that all nursing home residents receive a comprehensive and uniform assessment. Fulfillment of this requirement allows for the collection of standard assessment data on every resident, thereby producing a vast body of information about the characteristics of nursing home residents and how they change while receiving long-term care.

Clearly, it has been a major undertaking to install a national resident assessment system in 16,000 nursing homes. The effort has required determining the standard data to be collected, designing and testing techniques for collecting it reliably, and training professionals to conduct the routine assessments. The project has taken several years to implement, but the effort is—and will be—extremely valuable.

In fact, long-term care providers have enthusiastically supported the development of this national resident assessment data base because we feel certain that the data collected will serve as the basis for development of a reliable quality assessment tool that will be able to measure patient outcomes and, therefore, the quality of care.

CONCLUSION

As policymakers continue to focus on the establishment of effective quality assurance programs, it is essential that they recognize that regulations alone are not the answer. Their success in dealing with the more difficult issues of resource availability will determine how effective we are as a nation in assuring that quality long-term care will be available to the growing number of Americans who need it. Only after these more fundamental issues of delivering quality care are addressed can we begin to measure quality in a meaningful way.

4

OBRA as a Measure of Quality

Paul R. Wilging

The Omnibus Budget Reconciliation Act of 1987 is an interesting development in the march toward enhanced quality of care, at least as it relates to the institutional side of long-term care.

OBRA can be looked upon as the very best hope in terms of practical legislative activity intended to improve the quality of care in long-term care facilities. We must, however, begin to apply fiscal and political realities to this legislation. OBRA contains approximately 50 pages called the "Nursing Home Reform Act of 1987." I think by everyone's estimation, it is a critical piece of legislation for nursing homes. It has been looked upon by consumers, providers, and lawmakers alike as a promise, an opportunity. It may be difficult to believe, but the long-term care industry has largely supported OBRA. Many people have assumed that since the law was designed to enhance the quality of care and placed new requirements on long-term care facilities, that long-term care providers must be against it.

What many people fail to realize, however, is that long-term care providers favor programs that are good for our residents. We had questions about some parts of the law, but overall we were supportive of provisions dealing with quality assurance and quality care. We worked closely with consumers in The National Citizens' Coalition for Nursing Home Reform and a number of other groups in Washington, D.C. A good bill was passed. We saw it as a compilation of the best practices that were already being performed in the best facilities across the country. I think at the core of OBRA is a recognition of the need for a definition of quality in long-term care. It is unfortunate that we had to wait for Congress to describe what quality long-term care should be about, but at least Congress gave us a starting point.

OBRA says that the long-term care facility's purpose is to bring each resident to the highest practicable level of mental, physical, and psychosocial well-being, and to do so in an environment that emphasizes residents' rights. To do this, the facility's focus must be on quality of life as well as quality of care. I think this definition reflects the best of what has been going on in nursing homes across the country. For the first time in the history of nursing home regulation, Congress has recognized that there are a number of determinants of quality and that the system up to that point had focused only on a few of them. Up to the point of OBRA, the regulatory system was mostly punitive in nature rather than encouraging facility operators to provide higher quality care.

OBRA was the watershed. It did not move away totally from the punitive approach, but it complemented it. What OBRA said, from my perspective, is that attitude and motivation in nursing facilities are necessary but not sufficient as far as quality of care is concerned. Absent attitude and motivation, we cannot ensure quality care. Attitude and motivation alone, however, will not guarantee quality care. There are two other critical determinants: resources and training. Only through better training, more adequate compensation, and self-regulation to shore up the marks of professionalization will nursing home care live down its current reputation. *That is exactly what OBRA did.* It recognized, to some extent prodded by the industry, that there is more than attitude and motivation necessary if we are going to enhance the quality of institutional long-term care.

Embedded in OBRA is a phrase which says that state Medicaid programs must adjust their rates to accommodate the new OBRA standards. This was the first time in the history of the Medicaid program that such language had ever been included in legislation. Also in the law are eight new remedies that can be levied by either federal or state governments on nursing facilities who do not, for whatever reasons, meet the requirements of the law. These remedies include termination, a ban on further admissions, civil fines, and receivership. One of the nursing home industry's real successes was in reaching agreement to change the vocabulary of "enforcement." We now use the word "remedy" rather than "penalty." The vocabulary is important because it sets the tone for the regulatory process. Regulation must strike a delicate balance between the control necessary to achieve a basic standard and the degree of professional discretion which will allow a nursing home to respond to the residents' needs.

OBRA did provide a tool that will help caregivers bring residents to—and maintain them at—their highest practicable level of physical, mental, and psychosocial well-being. This tool is the *resident assessment process.* The law requires that within 14 days of admission, and at least annually thereafter, nursing facility staff must perform a comprehensive, interdisciplinary assessment of every resident and that a care plan must be developed from that assessment. Plans of care are used by the facility staff to track success in bringing residents to their highest practicable level of functioning. The resident assessment process was largely based on what has already been happening successfully in nursing facilities in this country. The Institute of Medicine panel, which helped craft OBRA, was very impressed with a program being used by a national nursing home chain. What is critical to understand about this part of the law is that the resident assessment process requires adequate resources.

It is important to note that parts of OBRA dealing with residents' rights are more a function of attitude and motivation than of resources. Treating residents as customers, treating residents with basic human dignity is not something that requires additional resources. It may take some staff training, but it does not require a major financial commitment.

Another important question is whether OBRA is likely to fulfill its promise. *Highest practicable level of functioning* was defined as it relates to the individual resident. What I see happening across the country is a not so subtle transformation in terms of the parameters of that definition. Highest practicable is being defined in terms of the fiscal pressures within the facility.

An important question must be asked of health care providers: what does highest practicable mean to you? When I visit facilities, I ask the director of nursing how many hours a week of physical therapy is provided for the average resident. After being given the answer, I ask a second question: how many hours of physical therapy would be appropriate to make a measurable difference in bringing a resident to the highest practicable level of functioning. The answer I get to the second question is invariably two to three times higher than the first number. If we go through all of the other therapeutic interventions, we see the same thing.

The issue of staff-to-resident ratios is also critical. In acute care, for every 100 patients, there are 98 registered nurses. In nursing homes, however, there are 5.2 nurses for every 100 residents. Why do we see such a difference? Is it because the acuity levels of nursing facility residents do not require such a ratio? Or is it because we are defining "highest practicable" within the context of resource availability. I believe that fiscal and political realities are governing our definition of "highest practicable." In fact, fiscal and political realities are driving OBRA implementation.

The situation in California is a case in point. Approximately three and one-half years after OBRA was enacted, the state of California began to realize the implications of the legislation. In early 1991, California state officials suggested that the state was already meeting standards equivalent to OBRA and, therefore, there was no need for California to do anything different as far as nursing home care was concerned. State officials instructed the Director of Certification not to change the approach to surveying nursing homes in the state. The state officials also submitted to the federal government an amendment to its Medicaid plan, as required by law, which claimed that state laws were equivalent to OBRA. In response, the National Senior Citizens' Law Center sued the state. When the HCFA (Health Care Financing Administration) administrator rejected the California approach, state and federal officials reached an agreement whereby the federal government agreed to change the "interpretive guidelines." This amounted to changing a few "shalls" to "shoulds" and changing a paragraph here and there. The final resolution of the California situation will tell us a great deal about how "highest practicable" will be defined.

Across the country, the increase in the reimbursement rate is averaging about $1.50 per resident. I contend that $1.50 is not what most people had in mind when they put the words "highest practicable" into law. While much of the best of OBRA costs us not one penny, important new or revised components of the OBRA regulations cannot be done for $1.50 per resident.

A facility that is now doing resident assessments that were not required previously is finding that it takes approximately three to four hours of registered nurse time to do each assessment. We are talking about a great deal of additional time and more sophisticated approaches to care planning which require highly trained nurses. The biggest issue in OBRA over the next few years will relate to the resources necessary to bring residents to—and maintain them at—their highest practicable level of functioning.

Providers have to use the judicial branch of government to obtain clarification. The American Health Care Association (AHCA) filed a lawsuit, which we may appeal, in which we sought to force the HHS (Health and Human Services) secretary to meet his responsibility to assure that the states are paying for OBRA. Although we have lost the first round of this battle, we feel it is critical to put pressure on the HHS secretary to fulfill his responsibilities by assessing the adequacy of what states will pay for OBRA. In another lawsuit which was filed in California, AHCA asked for—and was granted—the right to intervene. In effect, we will try to get the court to order the HHS secretary to look behind state assurances and to apply the definition of "highest practicable." Our goal is to be sure that the federal government has determined what "highest practicable" really means.

To reiterate, "highest practicable" is the heart and soul of OBRA. It is what the nursing home industry (i.e., long-term care) is all about; it is our mandate. It should also be our aspiration. Providers cannot do it alone, however. Federal and state governments have a key role to play in the successful implementation of OBRA.

5

Response to "OBRA as a Measure of Quality"

Mary Ousley

It has been said that it takes an experienced long-term care professional ten to 20 minutes to make a judgment about the quality of a nursing home operation. I think I have reduced that time to approximately three minutes. Having worked in long-term care as a member of a corporation that acquires and purchases nursing homes, and in my capacity, also, as an industry representative, I begin the evaluation on my way to the front door. The external environment offers hints as to what to expect inside. Once I open the door, however, it is my sense of smell and what I see that are my first and best clues. The next thing I look at is the staff interaction with the residents and with each other. My experience over the years has rarely found me in error with respect to that first impression and evaluation.

Much of what is contained in OBRA has been standard practice in many facilities for many, many years. Is OBRA an indicator of quality, a measure of quality? At this time, the answer is "no." I was part of a team of industry representatives that worked with the staff of the Health Care Financing Administration (HCFA) on the policy and regulatory aspects of OBRA. Three years later, we still lack the final regulations and guidelines. This is not simply frustrating, it speaks to the pace, complexity, and inefficiencies of the bureaucratic process. As chairperson of the Facilities Standards Committee for the American

Health Care Association, I support the goals of this committee: to maintain regulatory oversight for what is happening within the industry, to work with the regulators, and to guide and direct the industry in its responses and initiatives.

I also know, in a perverse way, that despite the hours and hours given to create a piece of meaningful legislation which represents the interests of the client and the industry, many of my colleagues will feel that the industry team "sold them out." If OBRA is to be a measure of quality, then we must fully understand what happened in the past, prior to OBRA.

Three failures pointed to the need and provided momentum for an OBRA type of legislation. The primary failure was that the industry failed to define an optimal level of care. The second failure, clearly addressed in OBRA, was the survey and certification process. A survey system that is incapable of accurately evaluating a nursing home and is unable to assist a facility to reach and maintain compliance is an inadequate survey and certification system. If quality is measured, for example, by a tally of the number of patients who died, is a quality assurance system (i.e., survey) based on 32 indicators of care a better system? It is a well-known fact that the surveyors pre-OBRA were poorly trained and that subjectively based noncompliance determinations were the rule rather than the exception. The consumer guides published by special interest groups provided the media multiple opportunities for "industry bashing." An example is instructive. A recent consumer report revealed that in Kentucky, 10 percent of the facilities were noncompliant with regulations dealing with food storage. That same report indicated that Indiana, just across a bridge from Kentucky, had problems with food storage in 95 percent of its facilities. The issue of validity of findings clearly had to be raised. That particular consumer report demonstrated the inadequacies of the pre-OBRA system.

The third failure was the failure of government and society. Despite the seminars, conferences, and politicking which focus on what the industry needs to do and wants to do, there has been no commitment of the resources to meet the identified goals. Every study has demonstrated precisely what the Institute of Medicine report (1986) focused on: the delivery of care. Yet, the industry and the government focused on the policy manuals. It was rather as if a proper policy would guarantee good care. OBRA moves us away from an obsession with process and buildings and forces us to evaluate the actual outcomes of care. It also directs us to observe and emulate "good practice" within the field. The direction of change was toward resident rights, quality of care, and quality of life.

The *measure* of quality of care in OBRA was captured by the operational phrase "highest practicable," about which Wilging has written at length. I would like to suggest another way to capture outcomes of care: *positive harm* and *negative harm*. Prior to OBRA, the industry tended to evaluate care from the perspective of negative harm (i.e., patients should not be harmed, nothing bad should happen). The prevailing wisdom was that if nothing negative occurred, then a facility was in compliance with standards. Another way of describing negative harm is the example of a patient who is admitted to a nursing home and does not develop a pressure sore. Nothing bad happens, but nothing good necessarily happens either. Not developing a pressure sore may be good care but it is not sufficient. OBRA *attempts to ensure that residents do not experience "positive harm"* (i.e., failure of a resident to achieve the highest practicable level of function).

The notion of "highest practicable"—how it is defined and implemented in facilities—will be the most significant aspect of OBRA in its intent to assure quality outcomes. The core issue is that residents are not to deteriorate unless it is clearly shown (documented) that said deterioration was unavoidable. Outcomes of care will be identified through the resident assessment process and the instrument designed for that purpose. Longitudinal data collected by the instrument will indicate patterns, trends, and reasonable outcomes of care (i.e., the standards). The resident assessment and plan of care are a joint effort of resident, staff, and family such that the constituents of "good care" will be identified and agreed upon. Highest practicable, then, becomes a tangible, measurable outcome.

The resident assessment can be viewed as an aggressive, functional status measurement. The data generated by this process may, in fact, represent the future of professional nurse empowerment. It has been said that information is power and control. An alternate way of perceiving this aggressive assessment process lies in the data which suggest that the (assessed) resident has the capacity to "do" more. The practitioner, the administrator, can no longer ignore this data, this information. Something, some intervention or plan must be designed and delivered. It is no longer acceptable to cite insufficient resources as a reason for failure to provide the interventions necessary to bring the resident to the highest practicable level, a potential indicated by the assessment itself. Staff empowerment, then, is simultaneous with resident empowerment through the assessment process.

The attention given to resident rights through OBRA moves it away from a mere paper compliance activity done at the time of admission (i.e., the resident or family gets a list of rights, is given the opportunity to ask questions, and signs that said list has been reviewed and received). Resident rights under OBRA constitute an active responsibility for the facility, wherein administration and staff must assist and assure residents in the exercise of their rights. Dignity, choice, participation, and self-determination are key rights. The resident is to participate in facility decisions with respect to the environment and operational issues.

The quality assurance imperative is the overarching intent of the OBRA legislation. In what is still a cottage industry in many respects, long-term care facilities are now mandated to conduct meaningful assays of care with concrete plans of correction. In a sense, the nursing home is being told to know its problems in advance of the survey, that is, not to wait for the surveyor to arrive and point out the problems. The "remedies," the fines, are much more punitive if a facility has failed to identify a problematic area than if it has identified the problem on its own. The industry needs well-educated, trained professionals to meet the OBRA challenge. Every indication is that nursing homes want to be held accountable.

The wonder of OBRA is its scope and depth. The problem with OBRA is that its principles outreach the resources made available to realize its intent. The survey process of the future might be a team of peers who use the OBRA survey guidelines and methodology to help long-term care facilities meet the quality imperatives.

This change could have the salutary effect of moving the survey and certification process from a punitive one to one that is consultative. Some corporate chains are beginning to do this, voluntarily, even though they still have to go through the regulatory survey process. The issue, then, is not "to survey or not to survey" but an evaluation-of-care process that acknowledges the unique environments of long-term care facilities and the residents and staff who inhabit them.

REFERENCES

Institute of Medicine. (1986) *Improving the quality of care in nursing homes.* Washington, D.C.: National Academy Press.

6

The Future of Quality in Long-Term Care

Sheldon L. Goldberg

The quest for quality is a never-ending task in today's long-term care industry. While recent reforms have taken an important step forward in raising the standards of care in the nation's nursing homes, they should not be the last word on quality improvement. There are more ways to promote and measure quality than those found in the nursing home reform provisions of OBRA 1987, and professionals in the long-term care field need to seek them out and embrace them. Only then can this industry begin to roll back the negative image that has led to the current regulatory system.

OBRA REFORMS

Clearly, OBRA represents an important step forward in focusing the long-term care industry on quality. The law took the best standards of care already practiced in many nursing homes nationwide and made them the law of the land. Thanks to strong advocacy by the industry itself, the law provides a new definition of care in nursing facilities— the "highest practicable physical, mental, and psychosocial well-being of residents." "Highest practicable" is defined as the highest level of functioning and well-being possible, limited only by the individual's present functional status and potential for improvement. Facilities must ensure that each resident obtains optimal improvement and does not decline if the facility can prevent it.

In addition, for the first time, the survey process under OBRA recognizes something that long-term care professionals have known for years—that quality is not measured by paper compliance, but by talking with residents and seeing how their day-to-day care is progressing, and that outcome is the true test of quality. In this way, OBRA's quality-of-life requirements, especially those regarding residents' rights, will contribute to enhanced resident satisfaction in nursing facilities by putting renewed emphasis on the elderly themselves.

The long-term care industry has embraced OBRA as a new partnership among government, nursing facilities, and consumers designed to enhance the quality of care provided to the nation's senior citizens. Long before OBRA was enacted, many nursing facilities were already enthusiastically advocating many of its provisions. Many homes had already made significant strides; for example, in reducing the use of restraints.

While OBRA supports many of the quality improvements that were already occurring in nursing homes, it fails to recognize one of the most pressing realities of caring for the elderly in today's society— namely, economics. Most in the long-term care industry are committed to the highest possible care for residents, which OBRA has taken steps toward encouraging, but the government that enacted the law has not taken the responsibility for funding it. To ensure quality improvement, the federal and state governments, through Medicare and Medicaid, must provide the resources necessary for nursing facilities to carry out these reforms.

FUTURE EFFORTS

Clearly, OBRA is not the first step in quality improvement, nor is it the last. What the industry needs is a regulatory system built on a true partnership and which focuses even more on outcome rather than on paper compliance.

Accreditation

Improvement comes when the right attitude, environment, and conditions exist for it, not when it is mandated by law. To enhance quality, the long-term care industry needs a system that rewards excellence, instead of one that focuses all of its energy on penalizing those who break the rules. The fact is, a system that focuses on inspection and discipline does not promote quality but, instead, promotes defensive attitudes.

The American Association of Homes for the Aging (AAHA) believes that the establishment of an accreditation program is one such option for facilities to use to push the care frontier beyond OBRA. The goal ought to be a private accreditation system that is even more vigilant than the current regulatory system and which stimulates creativity and creates a true commitment to quality among facilities.

AAHA has already seen the accreditation process work successfully with its sponsorship of the Continuing Care Accreditation Commission. The accreditation process is rigorous and consumer-oriented, as its goal is to determine whether an applicant retirement community meets the highest standards of care. It involves extensive self-study by the facility's staff, board of directors, and residents—all of whom measure the facility against its stated mission and against established standards of excellence in the field. The process includes an on-site evaluation by trained and committed professionals and culminates in a review by a national commission.

The value of this voluntary process is that it is consultative, not punitive or adversarial, as the current system for long-term care facilities often is. Moreover, those communities that do not reach the standards necessary for accreditation are helped to do so, instead of being left to struggle with their problems alone.

Professionalism

The accreditation system for retirement communities also works because it is built upon a feeling of mutual respect among all professionals involved. Facilities are recognized as having good faith and a commitment to improvement, not because someone tells them they should, but because they want to provide the highest quality of care possible to their residents.

Care in long-term care facilities will improve when the people who provide that care are treated well and respected as professionals. The field needs more recognition for its professionals as well as incentives for others. It also needs more certification programs that raise the level of performance, education, and identity of the profession. AAHA is proud of its record in providing outstanding professional education year after year, but it recognizes that more needs to be done.

Total quality management (TQM) is one way many industries are already accomplishing this goal. TQM empowers every individual who works for an organization, encouraging each person to make decisions that promote a commitment to quality. For care to improve, each caregiver in a facility—from the administrator to the aide who bathes and feeds residents—must have in his or her heart a commitment to providing the highest quality services possible. This kind of commitment does not come from penalizing caregivers who do things incorrectly, but from creating a partnership that involves mutual respect. Under the current regulatory system, however, many long-term care professionals are forced to focus on how to provide the kind of care necessary to meet survey requirements, rather than focusing on the kind of care residents need.

Ethics

One of the hallmarks of a profession is a high ethical standard of practice. This means having a sense of corporate ethics that permeates every aspect of an organization and its people—from residents and families to the community it serves. Ethics is not something that is or can be mandated by OBRA or any other law but, rather, is something that must come from within every person at a facility.

AAHA is in the process of developing just such an ethical standard for its members—a corporate credo. The credo states clearly what AAHA members, as professionals in the long-term care field, aspire to: a dedication to providing quality services at reasonable costs; a commitment to providing a more meaningful life for all persons; a concerted effort toward promoting resident autonomy; and a strong desire to go beyond the minimum standards established by government. The credo will help facilities improve the quality of the care they provide by setting high standards toward which they can continually strive.

AAHA also recently joined with the American Association of Retired Persons in a project aimed at promoting ethical reflection in nursing homes through the establishment of ethics committees. AAHA firmly believes that through ethical review, long-term care facilities can enhance quality of care and protect the dignity and autonomy of those they serve.

CONCLUSION

It is time for the long-term care industry, hand in hand with consumers and professionals, to make a clear statement about its commitment to deliver superior care to our nation's elderly. It must do this not by merely accepting standards at the lowest common denominator, but by establishing a high standard to which everyone can aspire.

The industry, however, cannot do this alone. It needs the cooperation of other sectors in our society, particularly government. The federal and state governments, too, must live up to their responsibilities and do their fair share in improving care. It is not acceptable for the government to withhold, delay, or simply slash Medicare and Medicaid reimbursement to long-term care facilities. In many ways, the future of quality improvement in the nation's nursing facilities will be greatly affected by the present lack of clarity on how this society is going to pay for the long-term care needs of its citizens.

The key to improving quality in the long-term care industry is to give facilities the ability to manage for total quality rather than to manage for the survey process—and then to reimburse them fairly for the quality services they provide. Voluntary accreditation, the development of systems that promote professionalism, and the enmeshment of the industry in ethics all can make significant strides toward this goal. No law can do the same.

7

Response to "The Future of Quality in Long-Term Care"

Robert B. Friedland

At the Pepper Commission hearings (1988–1990), I had the opportunity to think about a health care and a long-term care system, but I also learned the reality of how difficult it is to reach a political consensus on what a fair system should be. I worked on and wrote about access to health care and long-term care. Once the recommendations of the commission were made, I traveled throughout the country explaining what the Pepper Commission had attempted to do—and why.

Through this experience, I came to realize that not all people in the country think alike about whether or not there is a basic right to health care. People were furious at the commission, and at me as the messenger. Everywhere I went, whether I was speaking to special interest groups that were politically on the right or on the left, business groups, labor groups, senior citizens—people were angry. The Pepper Commission either went too far or did not go far enough. For me, this was an important lesson.

Part of my role at the American Association for Retired Persons (AARP) is to direct health policy toward a fair and just health care system. Number one on our legislative agenda is the reform of the health care system to assure that all people of all ages have access to basic health care as well as to long-term care.

The passage of Medicare and Medicaid in 1964 brought with it many dilemmas. The general lack of attention to the Medicaid proposal and its coverage of long-term care or, rather, nursing home care, has been the root of most of our problems. The inclination to think of nursing homes as miniature hospitals and the fear of headline-grabbing catastrophe misled our legislators.

Things are not always as they appear and are not always that rational, but quick implementation of Medicaid meant that the states had to use the rules and resources that were readily available. The federal regulators did not know what to do. They looked to the rules and regulations that were available and what was readily available was the federal program for the construction of rural hospitals. The federal government seized upon these regulations; they were basically life safety regulations and rules about skilled nurse staffing ratios. Few nursing facilities at that time, even as long ago as 1964, could meet those standards. As a result, Medicaid was faced with a dilemma: the obligation to provide care for which there were no providers. This is a continuing problem even though political and regulatory ingenuity created the intermediate care facility with less stringent nursing staff requirements. The structural requirements, however, necessitated the building of new facilities. It was projected that it would be too expensive to simply refurbish the boarding care facilities that were the "nursing homes" at that time.

What we have now is a nursing home that very much looks like a mini-hospital; more of a hospital than a home, in fact. One could argue that the phrase "nursing home" is a misnomer in that such facilities provide little of either of the implied attributes of nursing care or home. The public has a very poor image of nursing homes. The nursing home is our last choice as a provider of care. The phrase "nursing home" conjures up images of abandonment, neglect, abuse, impoverishment, and fraud. A decade of headline-grabbing scandals after the enactment of Medicare and Medicaid only exacerbated that perception and confirmed the public's worst fears. The consequence of this nightmare perception of nursing homes was an outpouring of regulation, perhaps overregulation, mostly concerning staff credentialing, the width of corridors, and whether appropriate procedures were followed. There was little which focused on the actual care of the residents. To assure quality, nursing homes had become one of the most regulated industries in the country.

In a move to stem the tide of deregulation during the 1980s, Congress asked the Institute of Medicine (IOM) to study the status of nursing home regulations. The IOM findings and recommendations are the foundation of OBRA 1987, truly a watershed piece of legislation for the nursing home industry. The poor public image of nursing homes persists, however. Fortunately, conventional wisdom is, by and large, wrong. We, the professionals, know that, but we have to recognize how people feel.

As an industry, we are today where we should have been before Medicare and Medicaid were enacted. We are only beginning to define long-term care directly rather than derivatively (i.e., defining everything else and calling all that remains "long-term care"). We are beginning to define quality. As difficult as it is, we are trying to get to the root of what quality is. We now have some of the tools, such as the computer, which can be used to assess quality in terms of its impact on residents. By virtue of OBRA, we are beginning to shift the focus of nursing home regulations.

Wilging's paper and presentation offer us the strategy for assuring quality in the future. We simply need adequate resources. Medicaid reimbursement for nursing home care must be at a higher rate—or a rate commensurate with the costs of meeting the OBRA imperatives. Two questions were posed by Wilging: (1) how do we design a financing system that is humane and dignified while providing sufficient funding to ensure that all nursing home providers can deliver the highest quality of care possible in the most efficient way? and (2), to what extent can federal policy help alleviate the current shortage of nursing personnel in the nursing home setting? Wilging answered the first question by stating that we need to revamp the current financing system. I agree. Given the current federal budget deficit, however, Wilging (American Health Care Association) supports the expansion of private insurance initiatives.

What would private long-term care insurance do to alleviate the budget crunch in long-term care? It would remove from state Medicaid programs the ability to cut eligibility (for participation in the Medicaid Program) or reimbursement and allow states to seek to control their own budgets. While I agree completely with the first part of Wilging's solution (i.e., revamping the current financing system for long-term care) I am somewhat puzzled by his association's position. I suggest that if AHCA pushed for better public financing, that is, an elimination of Medicaid, that day would arrive sooner than the day when a sufficient proportion of the elderly population would have adequate private long-term care insurance such that Medicaid reimbursement would be insignificant for most nursing homes.

As to the second question, about the nursing shortage, AHCA offers both a short-term and a long-term solution. In the short run, Medicaid must properly reimburse nursing homes such that their nurses' salaries are on a par with hospital nurses' salaries and benefits. A long-term solution would be to encourage the training of geriatric nurses. On this point, I am in complete agreement: wages and benefits must be improved not only for nurses but also for nurse aides.

There is little doubt that the level of compensation and a recognized career ladder could have a substantial impact on recruitment and retention of nursing personnel, and ultimately quality of care. The position that nursing staff salaries need enhancement would be strengthened if we could demonstrate the critical relationship between Medicaid reimbursement and actual employee compensation.

While it is clear that there is a positive correlation between Medicaid reimbursement and private payers, we do not know the strength of that correlation. The correlation is not sufficient, however, since presumably, if Medicaid is paying too little, then private payers are paying too much. It is difficult to accept on face value the assertion that the nursing home industry is suffering financially when 75 percent of the industry is proprietary. Obviously, nursing homes are earning a sufficient rate of return on equity to attract some capital. A question which begs an answer is the degree to which the rates of return are "just sufficient" relative to the degree of risk to attract investment.

More money is needed, without question. Medicaid reimbursement rates are probably, on average, too low. Assurances are needed, however, that additional monies go to staff, and that the public sector is not inappropriately subsidizing the rates of return to the nursing home owner.

Most long-term care is provided in the home by the family and relatives. What we see in the public accounting, however, is what we pay for nursing home care. The growing demand for long-term care will ensure that the issues raised by Wilging et al. will be addressed. I am optimistic that the response to the growing demand will be in a relatively rational manner rather than by default. I say this with some degree of confidence because over the next decade corporate upper management and key advisors to Congress and the administration at federal and state levels will be themselves facing long-term care directly or indirectly through the avenue of their own families.

We have already seen a substantial shift. People are beginning to talk about the fact that they have a relative who needs assistance. People are talking about "caregiving"—this is a big step.

Companies have started to formalize "elder care benefits." The fact that we are at a crossroad in the policy decisions about long-term health care can also be seen in health services research. There has been a dramatic shift in the past few years toward questions of "outcomes." This is due, I believe, to advances in computer technology which enable such analyses—with federally funded support. Outcomes research is about averages (i.e., actual averages versus predicted events). These are difficult concepts. We have yet to fully identify and name all of the pieces. It is significant to note that health services research has major funding and support at the federal level.

The fact that major policy initiatives tend to get decided within the context of budget reconciliation, and always at the midnight hour, needs special attention. This was true for the new nursing home regulations, the Omnibus Budget Reconciliation Act. The spirit of OBRA prevails in that it has moved the nursing home industry in the proper direction. The resident assessment (i.e., Minimum Data Set) can make better care a reality by using the findings of properly conducted health services research.

With appropriate data and computer technology, we can, for example, provide feedback to nurse aides whereby they can understand that even though the person they are caring for is deteriorating, the deterioration is less than it would have been if the nurse aide had not intervened. This not only humanizes the computer technocracy, but it combines the principles of adult education, caregiving, feedback systems, motivation theory, and society's commitment to care for its older people.

8

Breaking Out of the Skinner Box

Pamela J. Maraldo

THE QUALITY PROBLEM

Throughout the 1980s, consumer groups and the press exposed hazards and poor quality care that were declared endemic to the long-term care industry. Resultant public outrage inspired a host of regulations and policy from federal and state agencies. In 1989, the Health Care Financing Administration (HCFA) released a 75-volume, state-by-state investigation of the nation's 15,000 nursing homes with less than impressive findings. Only 2,300 homes met minimum standards on 32 measures of the quality of care, from cleanliness and privacy to prompt care of bedsores and proper administration of medications. Nursing homes passed muster in the HCFA study only on meeting standards that should never have been an issue—such as the availability of emergency care and the absence of mental and physical abuse against patients.

As pervasive as it was, the quality problem was far from intractable. Yet today long-term care providers struggling with the urgent task of regulatory responsiveness, change, and innovation do so in a climate of public skepticism that creates unusual challenges. Ironically, the muckraking of the 1980s makes solving the quality problem more difficult in the 1990s. If—and indeed when—the long-term care industry succeeds in surmounting today's immense challenges, it will earn a powerful place in a higher quality health care delivery system of the future. But that remains to be seen.

BREAKING OUT OF THE SKINNER BOX

One reason real solutions elude us is this: policy implemented over the past decade to address the quality problem has been piecemeal regulation, not a comprehensive agenda for moving forward. As a result, the actions taken to solve the nursing home problem are now themselves problematic; they stand in the way of substantial progress that will ensure a good future for the industry—and for the millions of health care consumers dependent upon it.

The current legislative approach to achieving quality in long-term care has been decidely Skinnerian as well. The father of behavioral psychology, B.F. Skinner, pioneered the concept of positive reinforcement as a more efficacious developmental tool than negative reprisal—a philosophy that is instructive as policymakers approach the long-term care industry, which until now has been punished for egregious errors but not encouraged to extend itself beyond the realm of the mediocre.

Skinner developed the famous concept of the "Skinner Box," wherein theoretically an infant would live in an environmentally controlled area that met all of his or her physical needs, and when the child emerged he or she would not be inordinately frozen by fear and would respond fruitfully to opportunities to demonstrate excellence. Skinner used animal experimentation to argue that the wonder and creativity of the spirit are natural—they arise in those released from the Skinner Box with no prior socialization; the tendency toward mediocrity, on the other hand, is not natural but is nurtured through the constant negative reinforcement that is the norm in human development.

The long-term care industry must similarly break out of its own Skinner Box, and policymakers and health insiders must respond with positive feedback for the industry's movement toward exemplary quality—not episodic regulatory measures that are punitive. Indeed, long accustomed to having its financial needs more or less automatically met, the long-term care industry now faces a new era when it must, to satisfy its expanding need, recreate itself. In effect as in practice, long-term care providers must take the reins and not rely solely on government to create regulations that "force" quality. This is a negative reinforcement that will not bring the industry beyond its tremulous position at the fringe of satisfactory performance. Nor should the industry look to colleague health providers and policymakers to make them adjust to radically changing consumer demands for new standards of care—they might help, but it is the long-term care industry itself that must assume leadership.

THE REGULATORY QUAGMIRE

Under the regulatory agenda of policy in long-term care, when quality deteriorates enough, then government, at the urging of special interest groups like the American Association of Retired Persons (AARP), takes action. Such action, motivated as much by political as quality-of-care concerns, arises in a fragmented series of regulations, enforcing one tedious provision after another, which is more often than not too little too late. Even the Omnibus Budget Reconciliation Act (OBRA), which in its process of assembling all the fragments of health policy into one budgetary document ought to have set forth some semblance of a coherent agenda, instead called for regulating according to a few minimally acceptable standards of quality, a mark below which thou shall not go.

For example, one of the most important mandates in OBRA calls for a minimum of one registered nurse (RN) present on each shift. From the perspective of the average nursing home, which often enough has failed to meet this standard (leaving a licensed practical nurse in charge), this OBRA requirement is a giant step forward. By any other health industry standard of practice, however, and certainly from a consumer point of view, the "one RN" requirement hardly inspires confidence that quality is a top priority concern in America's nursing homes.

Other government mandates in OBRA similarly add up to the casting of a minimal safety net on the industry, requiring basic training requirements for nurse's aides and a new patient classification system. Government mandates are perfect examples of Skinnerian "negative reinforcement"—they punish the industry for poor past performance, but fail to offer constructive approaches to building a quality environment. Nor is the implementation problem borne by the long-term care industry alone. OBRA mandates are so ambiguously constructed that the Health Care Financing Administration has yet to issue regulations to offer the industry guidelines for following the mandates.

CREATING AN AGENDA FOR QUALITY

To be sure, OBRA minimum standards are better than nothing. But for an industry which serves such a critical role in the lives of millions of Americans, minimum is simply not good enough. The long-term care industry—and indeed the entire health care delivery system—will need excellence—not mediocrity—to satisfy its grave responsibility to the public. Policymaking in long-term care must, at its foundation, bring a philosophical commitment to quality as indivisible from our healthcare culture, and a commitment to creating a consumer-driven health care system.

How do we get there? Before we can create an agenda for quality in the long-term care industry, we must, as providers, administrators, policymakers, and consumers, develop some working consensus on the basic issue of what we hope to achieve in long-term care. What goals do we share? What should our health care delivery system accomplish and how does long-term care fit in? The Ross Laboratories/ National League for Nursing Long-Term Care annual invitational conferences have been of national import precisely because we have come together from a wide variety of interested perspectives to hammer out these extraordinarily complex, fundamental questions that can put us on the path to quality.

In the context of the big picture in health care, it is fair to argue that the problems in long-term care are not entirely the fault of the industry itself. Long-term care administrators and advocates deserve some credit for staying afloat amid the nursing shortage—which hit nursing homes twice as hard as hospitals—and for assuming responsibility for daunting new regulatory provisions that arose with little support and consultation for implementers.

THE NURSING SHORTAGE

Efforts to stem the nursing shortage have generated positive prospects for a solution in the future, although the shortage is still a major problem particularly in the long-term care sector. After years of precipitous decline, National League for Nursing preliminary 1991 data show dramatic increases in nursing school enrollments over the past two years, including unprecedented numbers in associate degree programs which have traditionally been the most frequent purveyors of talent to the long-term care industry.

However, patient demand for nursing services promises to accelerate much more quickly as the Baby Boomers age and technological innovations help produce new populations of the chronically ill. Few health industry sectors will be as hard-hit by the gap between supply of nurses and demand for their services as the long-term care industry. According to the report of the Health and Human Services Secretary's Commission on Nursing in 1988 and numerous other investigations, the key to permanently solving the shortage will be appropriate utilization of nursing services. Much progress has been made toward this important goal, and more remains to be accomplished as the years unfold.

LOW FEDERAL PRIORITY ON
LONG-TERM CARE

During much of the 1980s, the problems in the quality of the nation's long-term services took center stage in public concerns about health care as a whole. Despite the growing needs of an increasing population of elderly and chronically ill, long-term care continues to take a back seat to other segments of the delivery system in terms of support on the public and private levels.

Long-term care is marginalized because the health system still functions with an inordinate bias toward the acute-care medical model. As a result, the policymaking agenda fails to address the predominate health needs of the nation, and instead focuses on the episodic goals of curing incidents of disease and injury. With due respect to the achievements of medical science, as a central model for ordering priorities in health care it is inadequate. Long-term care—with its central objectives of *caring* and not usually *curing*, per se—is an excellent example of an extremely vital health issue neglected by the bias toward cure. Nor is long-term care alone among the pressing problems exacerbated by this fundamental emphasis on the medical model. Troubling trends indicative of our overreliance on the medical perspective for setting health policy arise in many other contexts.

THE TECHNOLOGICAL IMPERATIVE

Foremost among such trends as mentioned above is the overuse of technology. Economist Victor Fuchs wrote that "if the technology exists we must use it—regardless of the patient's wishes, regardless of the family's wishes, regardless of its effectiveness." The sequel to the Fuchs axiom is that physicians feel compelled to use all the technology that exists and patients are often compelled to go along with their wishes. Efforts are not often spared, no matter how unpromising. The respirators, heart machines, CAT scanners, and surgical procedures available to modern medicine are launched into action regardless of the prospects of success or even the prior track record of effectiveness. Congressional attempts to encourage the use of statistical data on the efficacy of a given procedure is condemned by physicians as "cookbook medicine."*

---

* In all fairness to MDs, the fear of lawsuits (i.e., litigious society) often drives their clinical decision-making and diagnostics.

"Cookbook medicine" or not, overuse of technology generates tremendous cost. And available numbers shatter the concept that the system works to the overall advantage of the nation's health. For instance, one-third of Medicare dollars are spent on life-sustaining technology in the last year of life in individuals over 80 years of age, while only 1 percent of the health care dollar is spent on prevention. Again and again the health care system senselessly buckles under to the resurgence of preventable epidemics and diseases.

In the United States, more high-technology equipment is used and more per capita on health care is spent than any other nation. In 1990, health costs ate an estimated $650 billion, nearly 12 percent of our GNP, and costs are expected to rise for 1991. Yet too little of the nation's enormous investment in health care is distributed to those most in need of it; 37 million Americans lack access to care, millions of elderly Americans are impoverished by health costs, and inattention to preventative health needs has resulted in unnecessary suffering and long lines at emergency rooms.

For the long-term care industry, a look at larger issues of health policy can seem somewhat ethereal when contrasted with the harsh fiscal realities of day-to-day operations. Furthermore, understanding that the climate of health policy in the nation does not place a priority on long-term care, and intervenes only when quality is poor, hardly inspires confidence that better times are ahead. Yet for industry leaders willing to look at the bigger picture and move forward accordingly, the future is bright indeed.

UNLIMITED POSSIBILITIES

Providers must courageously forge a new future without fear or the complacency of a guaranteed income—they must emerge and demonstrate the enormous potential of the determined human spirit. Just as Skinner contended that the possibilities for human development have barely been tapped, so too have we underestimated the ability of the long-term care industry to emerge as a vibrant, cutting edge force in American health care.

9

Assuring Quality in Long-Term Care: The Private Sector Approach

Maria Mitchell

It is clear that the government regulatory approach is not working in health care. Even at its best, it's far from ideal. What's worse, three years have passed since the nursing home reform legislation was signed into law, and the federal government has yet to implement the statute. The failure on the part of the regulators to act sums up the inadequacy of the governmental approach. On the other hand, the industry itself acknowledges that it has not done a very good job at policing itself either. Clearly, new solutions are needed.

Historically, what has happened in this country is that when market failure occurs in a particular industry, the government steps in as "social regulator." It is obvious that there was market failure when the federal government found it necessary to step in and introduce minimal safety requirements for nursing home care. When you look at OBRA, which contains such basic requirements as guiding the use of physical or pharmacological restraints and 24-hour nursing and client rights—these are regulations that the industry should have mandated for itself over the past 30 years. OBRA may be a watershed, but the fact that this kind of statutory mandate was necessary on the eve of the 21st century and long after the publicized nursing home scandals suggests that we still have a long way to go. Few would consider OBRA as visionary with respect to quality improvement.

53

The industry must look to itself first and foremost if it is to be visionary.

The state of American business today offers many analogies and lessons for the long-term care industry. Whether we talk about the terrible shape of the economy, or the crisis in the quality of products and services, the American business community must take much of the responsibility for creating this declining economic situation. Complacency, greed, and blind pursuit of profit has finally caught up with American industry as they have lost to foreign markets. We in this country are quick to give the Japanese credit for setting high standards of quality. Conversely, we also blame them for the failure of American business. But, it's far more complicated than that, and in large measure, American business has only itself to blame for its decline.

For years, American business did do things very well. American products represented the mark of excellence and set the world standard. At first, international competition did not pose a threat and profits soared. But growing competition from abroad actually caught us by surprise. It was not just that Japanese industry produced higher quality, less expensive, more fuel efficient cars, it was a globalization of the world-wide economy which brought foreign products from Japan, Germany, and other European, Asian, and Latin American countries flooding onto American shores. American businesses were caught off guard and were unprepared for the onslaught. For the first time, the worldwide leadership of American industry was challenged by fierce global competition. There were two choices for U.S. business leaders. They could rely on ingenuity to make a better product and improve lagging productivity. Or, they could cut costs and make a less expensive, inferior product. Sadly, we all know that they chose the latter route. The result is that the long run growth in productivity remains just under 1 percent, where it has remained for about 25 years since the late 1960s.

Leading analysts and commentators point to the fact that innovation is the key to success and American managers simply failed to keep up. People forget that the nation of Japan looked to a lot of early American innovations as a source for their quality improvements. Bluestone and Harrison talk about this in their book *The Great U-Turn*.

I do not think anyone would really disagree with the fact that American industry failed to innovate, and, when faced with the need to do so, could not figure out how to produce new products, improve the quality of the old ones, or even better market the products that they did have. And thinking about it, in retrospect, it sounds a lot like the nursing home industry. Nobody seems to know how to create a new product. We have had the same product for a long time. What is worse is that we do not know how to market the existing nursing home in a way that changes the reprehensible public perception of the long-term care industry.

Bluestone and Harrison contend that a major part of the problem in American industry is this: CEOs in American business have changed. The financial wizards and lawyers who are running companies do not have the experience or understanding of production and do not know what is going on down in the trenches. These CEOs direct their energies to enhancing short-term profits. No one is paying attention to the long term. As Hayes and Abernathy point out in their seminal work in the *Harvard Business Review,* true success really depends on an organizational commitment to compete over the long haul by offering a superior product.

It is easy to argue that the nursing home industry and the entire health care industry for that matter is pretty much in the same place that American business was 20 years ago. The nursing home industry basically grew out of itself and was the only game in town, in this particular arena. But like the business industry, people became complacent; they did not pay attention to quality and there was generally no competition to force them to do so. The result, as we know, is market failure from a public perception standpoint.

It has been suggested that the "dumping" syndrome on the part of families helped to create the unfavorable perception of the nursing home industry. I have to say from my own experience with CHAP, making home visits to patients, I heard repeatedly from elderly patients and their families that the reason they are so happy to be receiving care in the home is that they'd do anything to avoid going to a nursing home. That's not to say that that perception is a correct one, and that there aren't many good places to be, but the perception is very real, and is something that needs to be dealt with.

It is this public cry for change that really has pushed the industry to another level. We have all seen a major change in the consumer's role in health care, and this is certainly true with respect to nursing homes.

Ronald Inglehart at the University of Michigan has done a study on "culture shift" which basically addresses the change in what people expect and value. Over the last 20 years, Inglehart argues, American culture in particular, and most western cultures, have moved away from an obsession with economic growth and are becoming increasingly interested in the *quality* of life. Coupled with this change in what people want out of life is a significant shift in the distribution of political skills. More than ever before, people are taking an active interest in, and developing an understanding of, the political system. We have nevèr before had such an educated public. A public with a strong desire to participate in decision making and policy making can influence improvements in the quality of their own lives and the lives of people around them. These developments give us a good idea of why the consumer has taken such an active role in health care and nursing home care in particular—and that's not going to change. The consumer is only growing stronger in his or her advocacy for quality of life, and will take an increasingly active role in policy making and decision making.

What is going to happen to the baby boomers when they come of nursing home age? At present, you have a younger generation fighting on behalf of an older generation. Soon, we're going to have an older, vocal generation with the education, political savvy, and a clearly articulated notion of quality, fighting for themselves, their spouses, and their peers. We are only at the crest of this consumer trend toward demanding a better nursing home product. How we achieve a better product is really at the crux of any choice we make about the future.

The long-term care industry has not been as proactive in this regard as it could be. The prevailing wisdom is that any change for the better has been the result of dogged determination on the part of consumers. When you're constantly trying to catch up, it's hard to stay ahead. The key to generating a better product, as Bluestone, Hayes, Abernathy, and Inglehart have said, is through innovation. With the speed of technological developments, the status quo is not good enough. People have to look to innovative, creative ways to do things in order to make a better quality product, a better mousetrap. This is what the nursing home industry really needs to do: create and market a better product that really changes the public's perception about nursing homes. Whatever that product is, it has to come from the industry itself. The industry has to look to itself. Part of the problem with

OBRA's regulatory approach to quality improvement and the reasons why it will never fully change the public's perception of the industry is that the OBRA changes were initiated by consumers. It was the consumer who took the lead in making things different and better. Even though the industry supports OBRA and thinks it is a good thing, the fact is that the changes did not come from the industry but from outside the industry. The public perception is that the changes associated with OBRA were forced upon the long-term care industry.

In looking at innovation, then, how can this industry satisfy the consumer? How can we create a better product? Clearly, the private sector can play an important role: (1) through an accreditation process which will assure the public of quality improvements; (2) in the promotion of innovation through consumer based standards; and (3) ultimately, in strengthening the industry. It is striking to compare the attitudes which the nursing home industry has with respect to problems in the regulatory and governmental survey process in contrast to all the things that CHAP* as an accrediting body has set out to do. CHAP has strived to change the status quo of certification/accreditation as it exists in governmental regulation—to show how different and innovative a private approach can be.

While support of a private sector approach to accreditation, as a substitute for regulatory oversight, may be a desirable option, I would argue that there is much more to private sector accreditation than simply getting the government off your backs. A private sector approach to quality can result in building a better mousetrap, making a better product, and helping consumers and customers really understand what you do. At CHAP, we have seen it happen. The process is exciting, progressive, and positive. CHAP has been innovative from its inception. The Board is comprised of people who provide, people who receive, and people who pay for health care. This broad representation of consumers, payors, businesses, and providers gets at the issue that Dr. Fretwell addressed, the "either/or" issue.

It is not either you do a better job or we'll do a better job. It is all the parties coming together saying, "we all have responsibility for doing a better job, and how can we do things differently." Immediately, then, right at the start, the composition of the CHAP Board eliminates a

---

* Community Health Accreditation Process

major problem by bringing together the various parties who have a clear stake in defining quality and figuring out the best way to proceed. The goal of CHAP or any private accrediting body, or really any approach to quality improvement, should not be to set minimum standards or standards that are generally accepted within the industry, but to set higher standards that push the industry to a place where it did not think it could get to (or where it maybe cannot get to the first time around, but will the second time). That is really the whole idea behind the notion of total quality improvement: to keep improving beyond the point where you didn't think you could go.

In creating the CHAP program, we looked at the theories and concepts of total quality improvement, based on the now very familiar Deming approach, as well as all the other quality literature. When you are looking at a total quality improvement system, you don't just look at quality assurance, you look at the whole organization: that is what the CHAP standards address. We look at an organization's management and its finances. We look for ways to help organizations do a better job. The idea is to check to see whether people have the tools to provide the kind of care, and the kinds of services, that consumers are really looking for. Our standards focus very heavily on the financial component of the organization and its prospects for long-term viability.

We have CPAs, as well as nurses, that do site visits. In so far as providing organizations with tools, in conjunction with financial experts in home care, CHAP developed a scoring model to predict bankruptcy in home care which was based on Altman's "Z" score that was designed to predict bankruptcy in the banking industry. Essentially, we have a predictor for a home care organization's long-term financial viability and are in the process of creating another score that will predict financial viability in the short term.

In our view, you cannot provide good quality care unless you have the resources to do it and unless you have good management. We spend a significant amount of time examining an organization's management. The CHAP accreditation process is completely different from the stories we've heard about surveyors locking themselves in rooms and looking at policy and procedure manuals. Our site visitors spend most of the time talking to people, talking to staff at all levels, talking to managers, to people who really understand quality, and to people who understand what the process for achieving quality in all aspects of the organization is about. Seeking innovative ways to help the home care industry, we do not simply walk in with a big stick to identify things done incorrectly.

We go into homes and talk to patients receiving care. We also telephone discharged clients who are no longer dependent on the organization for service and therefore don't have fears about retribution if they tell the truth about the care they received. We also talk to vendors not only to ascertain the organization's reputation in the business community but also to assure that the organization extends the same quality service to its business customers as it does to its clients.

CHAP does not use the same terminology as the nursing home industry with respect to surveys. We don't even call them surveys—we call them "site visits"; and we don't use surveyors—we use "site visitors." This removes some of the negative and punitive connotations associated with the word "survey." "Visit" on the other hand implies a collegial, consultative approach where both strengths and weaknesses can be identified. Selecting the right people to conduct the visits and provide broad organizational expertise in the areas covered by the CHAP standards is a demanding task and something that we spend a considerable time assessing and monitoring. We do not just look at educational credentials but the breadth of the site visitor's experience in the industry.

The CHAP site visitors are people who have managed and run home care organizations so that when they sit and talk to you about your organization and give advice, you respect them and listen to what they have to say. The site visitors spend three to four days in training during which time they are carefully observed for their skills, their knowledge of the industry, and how they interact with others. We even observe each potential site visitor's presentation in mock exit conferences to see how he or she handles difficult situations. The time and effort it takes to select, train, and cultivate our site visitors is critically important; if one thing is true about the CHAP process, it is that it is only as good as its people. The site visitors have to be respected and trusted by the people in the organizations we accredit in order for the site visit to be a constructive process.

One of the first things that we tell our site visitors is that they enter an organization as an invited guest and should behave like they were going into somebody's home as an invited guest. We remind them that the organization has paid for their expertise, that they have voluntarily sought the highest standards of quality in the industry, and that this is their business, their livelihood, something that they do every day and take pride in, and that the site visitors must respect this and honor this. The site visitors are not there to simply look for what is wrong and talk about what is wrong, but also to point out what the organization is doing that is good, and what they should be proud of. When a problem is identified, the site visitors will offer sound advice on how to correct the problem, from the perspective of their own experience or what they have seen in other places. The site visitors do not just tell you that there is a problem because you are not meeting a standard written on a page in an accreditation manual.

The interesting thing is that, at the end of the site visit, there is an exit conference which most of the staff attend which is unlike other exit conferences where people come to hear the bad news. Our exit conferences are marked by a great sense of exhilaration because the entire accreditation process energizes and focuses the organization on doing a good job. The site visit has offered positive feedback on this good work and constructive advice on how to change the things that, by and large, the organization has already identified as a result of preparing for the visit and reviewing the standards. This constructive approach gives the organization a way to pull together and fix the problems while drawing on its own internal strengths.

I contend that this CHAP process is vastly different from anything that anybody has ever thought about, in terms of a survey process. Probably the best testament to the success of this process is in the evaluations. CHAP does not just take for granted that we are doing a good job. We ask the organizations (i.e., agencies) to evaluate the process, and we ask the site visitors to evaluate one another on an ongoing basis.

One of the questions on the evaluations is, "How can the process be improved?" In truth, more than once in the last six months, we've gotten back comments that state, "the process can't be improved, the process is great." I suspect there is nobody in long-term care that ever went through a survey process that even comes close to that kind of feedback. Several organizations have told us how things improved as a result of the process, how the shift to outcomes and away from structure and process has improved productivity and the quality of care. We have been told that nurses have informed their supervisors that as a result of CHAP, they go about providing care in a different way.

CHAP's financial consulting has also improved several organizations' bottom line. One agency said we saved them over four million dollars with the advice that they were given from the site visitor who was a CPA. It appears that CHAP is really making a difference, both in terms of quality and in terms of strengthening the organizations themselves.

Do not be misled, however, by this rosy depiction; we also have to be tough. When there are problems, we do not walk away from them. As a result, we have a much higher denial rate than other accrediting or certifying bodies. About 15 percent of the agencies we visit are not accredited the first time around. Interestingly enough, those people and organizations are among our biggest supporters, because they know that it is not a meaningless process; it is not a rubber stamp. With two exceptions in the past three years, all those organizations not originally accredited worked to the point where they were ultimately accredited, because it was something that they really wanted to do. You need to remember that, at this point in time, this is a voluntary process and does not take the place of governmental surveys.

This accreditation process, then, is really people working together to improve the system through innovation. Evidence of this is that CHAP was recently awarded a major grant from the W.K. Kellogg Foundation to develop outcome measures for home care, one of only two major studies nationwide in this industry. Different and unique about this study is that we are incorporating the consumer view into the definition of quality. Basically, we are assessing the consumers' notion of what care should be prior to care being given and then, when care is completed, seeing if such care met consumers' expectations and their needs.

At a number of different times throughout the process, we are determining what it is that the patient needs, and what the patient feels is quality care. This is an integral part of the outcome. Another major focus of this project is empowerment. Staff held focus groups at all the sites where we were conducting research. What they found is that if you empower your staff, they will empower their patients. A key factor in the new nursing home assessment tools is the fact that if you go to the trouble of finding out what the patient needs, you just can't walk away. You have to do something about it. Management can't walk away either if it goes to the trouble of finding out what their *staff's* needs are. The Kellogg project addresses both of these concerns *and* the link between the empowered staff and the empowered patients.

The project will provide a framework for agencies to compare the results of their activities with the other agencies participating in the project. So the fact is, we're looking at quality through consumers and empowerment and many other issues, and it really is extremely exciting.

One final issue in home care is hearing people talk about the fact that they are not paid for quality. You engage in a host of activities to assess, monitor, and improve quality and it doesn't "pay off." Facts tell us otherwise, however. There is a fair amount of evidence just in the example of American industry where quality does pay and where, if you don't have a quality product, you don't get anything. One of the things we are addressing in the Kellogg project is "outcome based reimbursement." We have already started discussions with the Health Care Financing Administration (HCFA) about changing the reimbursement system so that those organizations with better outcomes would be paid more. We believe this is very necessary. In the current reimbursement system, the incentives are wrong. The private sector is attempting to change these incentives. One of the most dramatic examples is taking place in Cleveland where a coalition of the local major businesses has joined with providers and hired an outside consultant to develop outcome measures that will be used to compare providers according to their outcomes. The information will be made public; the employers participating in the coalition will offer strong incentives in their employee benefit plans to select those organizations with the better outcomes. The "preferred provider" gains market share and the low-quality inefficient providers lose share. Quality *is* rewarded.

So it is happening in the private sector. CHAP is working to see that it also happens in the public sector. Nursing home providers say that they "survived" the survey system. What we like to say at CHAP is that it's not good enough to survive, you have to thrive and prosper. Our intent is to boost the health of home care organizations in today's rocky market place where mere survival really isn't good enough.

The prospects for the nursing home industry are somewhat bleaker as a result of bad public perception. Long-term care would benefit from a private sector approach to quality improvement that could really help achieve innovation with a strong consumer and management focus that would take it beyond survival. In the words of Carl Schramm, if CHAP didn't exist, someone would have to invent CHAP.

10

Response to "Assuring Quality in Long-Term Care: The Private Sector Approach"

Ethel L. Mitty

There are two aspects of the Community Health Accreditation Program (CHAP) which are in striking contrast to the accreditation (survey) process for institutional long-term care. The CHAP experience appears to be *nurturant* and *educational. This is quite different from the survey process for nursing homes.* In New York state, for example, the site visit staff of the department of health used to be known as "consultants/surveyors." With the implementation of the New York state quality assurance system (NYQAS), the word "consultant" was dropped from the title; the site visitors were known as, and acted as, "surveyors." Their role enactment is as opposite to nurturant as can be imagined.

WHAT CAN WE LEARN FROM THE CHAP PROCESS?

The CHAP process strikes me as a learning experience with educational outcomes; that is, you go to a seminar, the program outline states that "at the end of this course you will be able to do a, b, and c"; or it states that the "outcomes of this course will be x, y, and z." Mitchell

63

described CHAP as a "meaningful process." Experts from the community health domain itself are trained to do accreditation. Completely familiar with the context of practice, they are well equipped to evaluate performance and outcomes as well as provide guidance for improvement or correction of poor practice. Not at all adversarial, and clearly in a teaching mode, the CHAP process offers us a perspective on assessing quality which can be useful for institutional long-term care. We are driving ourselves crazy in long-term care trying to define "quality." Our approach, goal, and error is that we are conceptualizing quality as a fixed, immutable phenomenon. Fretwell addressed our society's obsession with either-or dualistic thinking. We are locking ourselves in to the same either-or trap with respect to quality, that is, that an outcome is a measure of quality or it is not; that an outcome meets a "level" of quality—like "highest practicable"—or it does not. If we place quality in the context of teaching and growth, however, and we accept that a quality-of-care outcome will be a "moving target," then we have an exciting opportunity to transform the quality imperatives of OBRA into educational imperatives.

MEANINGFULNESS IN ACCREDITATION AND SURVEY PROCESSES

The notion of "meaningfulness," as applied to CHAP, speaks to the concept of autonomy. Current literature on ethics, resident rights, and professional practice all address that key concept. Defined side by side, meaningfulness and autonomy both state that the ability to be involved in choices and decision making, no matter what the level, is *the* significant action. According to Bruce Vladeck, president of the United Hospital Fund, the definition of quality of life includes meaningful participation, choices. The philosopher and ethicist, Harry Moody, stated that autonomy means meaningful decision-participation. I find it remarkable that what OBRA is insisting on for residents of nursing homes, and what CHAP appears to be doing for those community health agencies which elect the CHAP accreditation process, is denied to long-term care facilities during their regulatory survey process.

The concept of meaningfulness needs to be incorporated into our language and construct of quality. The concept of "negotiated consent" was presented in a fairly recent Hastings Center Report in which it was suggested that negotiated consent should be the modus operandi for patient autonomy in treatment plan consent. I propose that we take a similar approach in surveying (accrediting) institutional long-term care. Given that there are no life safety or major quality-of-care deficiencies, the administrator/nursing director would negotiate with the surveyor, "this is what can be accomplished by such a point in time." If we can place the quality-of-care survey process in the context as described, then we can have an educational, meaningful survey process rather than the punitive experience it tends to be. A secondary gain of this kind of survey process is that it might restore nursing home staff self-respect and pride in the workplace. I make a particular point of this since many nursing home staff tend to think of themselves as second-class citizens who must be "policed" by government agencies to prevent them from acting abusively and unethically.

EMPOWERMENT

In closing this section of my commentary, I would also caution about the free-wheeling use of the word "empowerment." OBRA empowers the resident. The Minimum Data Set (MDS) assessment process empowers nursing, according to Ousley. I suggest that we consider the resident plan of care, derived from the MDS, as a negotiated decision between the caregiver and the care receiver rather than as a domain of power. It is uncomfortable for me to contemplate the plan of care as a force field where superordinate and subordinate vectors are exchanging positions. The phrase "empowerment" is an anathema to the humanistic, caring philosophy of nursing. Let us think of the care plan as the product of the resident/patient and nurse who have decided what the care plan will "look like" and what the (measurable) outcomes will be. Given the proper resources, the professional nurse—by definition accountable for practice—will obtain quality outcomes. It is almost redundant to treat the word "nurse" as different and separate from the phrase "quality of care."

INITIATIVES FOR QUALITY FROM THE PRIVATE SECTOR

While long-term care facilities are not reticent when it comes to legislative, financial, and regulatory issues, they are under-represented in the professional literature. This is attributable, without question, to the fact that facility administrators and nursing directors lack the time and the resources to put the proverbial pen to paper. There is no question, also, that excellent programs (and products) are in effect in nursing homes throughout the country. More often than not, members of academia write about issues, projects, and practices which they have initiated in nursing homes through joint ventures, student placement, and/or grant-supported operations.

The one exception appears to be in New York state through the NYQAS program which, through the agency of a highly reputable community organization (The Brookdale Institute) and a well-known acute-care center (The Mount Sinai Medical Center), encourages facilities to present their "best practices" at an annual symposium. Each year, a different care issue is selected: for example, incontinence and retraining, ambulation programs, restraint-free environments. The facilities are selected by peer review. These best practices receive scant attention from the press. Scandals sell more newspapers. A study of the art of public relations could well serve the industry in restoring and maintaining public confidence and pride in institutional long- term care.

THE ADVOCACY SECTOR

The Coalition for Nursing Home Reform analyzed the survey process in New York state. They found that there were more deficiencies cited in those facilities where the surveyors conducted more resident and staff interviews. (The survey process includes interview guidelines and questions for each Standard of Care.) The correlations were significant. The suggestion that the survey process was subjective and haphazardly conducted was thus established irrefutably. In keeping with its advocacy role, the coalition recommended that surveyors be given an award based on the number of deficiencies cited. In reflecting on my earlier remarks about the need for a meaningful survey experience from the facility staff perspective, I see that the award proposal of the coalition represents the quintessential deterioration of what was once a colleagial relationship between the surveyor/consultant and the nursing home.

BENEFITS OF PRIVATE SECTOR
INITIATIVES FOR QUALITY OF CARE

If the private sector is allowed to define and classify quality, the principles of *adult learning* can be applied to that process. What are some of the fundamental principles of adult learning with respect to the issue at hand? As a start, it means learning from one's mistakes. A cardinal tenet of adult learning is that the entry point, the learning point, is the point at which the student (receiver) wants to know something, to learn something. Information that the student does not want is not imposed on the student. The instructor is coming in at the interest point; instructor and student work together toward some mutually defined goal. It could be salutary for nursing home staff to know that they are involved in an educative venture, the quest for meaningful standards of care, rather than simply involved in a survey survival strategy called "quality."

The John Dewey approach to problem solving could also be applied to this elusive thing called "quality imperatives." Simply put, the problem is stated somewhat like "I have an itch." Ensuing steps describe the itch, what it looks like, its probable causes, and possible solutions—all in the context of that unique itch.

Wouldn't it be wonderful if the approach to quality was a *joint venture* between government, if you will, and the provider? (We will leave the consumer out of the formula for discussion purposes.) Instead of taking the dualistic approach which says "you did/did not do this; you have/have not complied with regulation x," the dialogue begins with "we have a mutual problem. . . ." This removes the "us-them" mentality and reactive behavior that characterizes facility response to regulations and survey. As private initiatives begin to assume some responsibility for the surveillance-of-care (i.e., quality) process in joint venture with the government/regulatory bodies, our mutual language has to use the "we."

OBRA's weakness is that it fails to recognize the professional code of ethics which demands accountability for practice. Instead, it reduces the professional role to that of a knee-jerk response to bureaucratic definitions of quality. If the private sector was allowed to assume a greater role in quality accountability, there just might be a significant *reduction in the operational costs of health delivery.* Also, *health services research* (HSR) might be appropriately funded *and* would draw on the expertise available within the professional community. The prevailing impression of research on quality is that there are lots of folks doing bits and pieces of research but there is no supraoperative putting it all together. The private sector, through its provider associations (e.g., AHCA, AAHA), could fill that role. These associations need to become more involved in, and invested with, the value and necessity for interinstitutional research.

By virtue of the MDS process, there will be masses of longitudinal data which will be invaluable in the construction of *thresholds of quality measures.* Using this data, we will be able to see patterns and trends of care needs and care outcomes for the individual resident, the facility, the sector of the country. This data must be merged with staffing and costs data; otherwise, any statement about quality will be meaningless. The inherent danger of these megaconstructs of quality is the tendency to apply to individuals what should only be applied to large quasi-homogeneous population groups.

The OBRA regulations clearly state that a resident has the right to refuse to consent to treatment. This regulation raises the issue of whether such a resident is still a "resident" who will be permitted to remain in the long-term care facility, using tax-supported resources. What is our obligation to the resident who refuses to accept what has been recommended?

I look forward to private sector initiated HSR that will finally identify and *validate the nursing staffing* by type and number that we need. It would not be surprising that, as a result of HSR, nursing homes will become designated as special care sites just as acute-care centers have been so designated—or allocated high-tech equipment. For reasons of sheer economic efficiency, we will probably see a distinction between nursing homes which manage residents with complex care needs such as dementia, rehabilitation, and so forth and those which offer palliative care.

With a research focus on quality, we will be able to identify candidates for *community discharge and managed care/case management*. One of the goals of the long-term care system is to maintain the individual at his or her maximum level of function in a safe, supportive environment. Cost aside, the best environment is out in the community. The reality of community residence for the frail elderly describes the burden and stress on the family caregiver (usually a female). The "respite bed" program is a way to increase the individual's potential to remain in the community. Yet, it has received insufficient financial support such that facilities are encouraged to create the respite bed. Findings from HSR can help identify candidates for respite care and their unique restorative education needs. This research might also describe those persons who would be unwilling to return to the community, thereby placing the facility at financial risk.

Two other research initiatives commend themselves. One concerns *substitutive function*, that is, the tasks/roles which could be assumed by a less costly worker, for example, registered nurse for doctor, practical nurse for registered nurse, nurse assistant for practical nurse or medication technician. A cost containment strategy which, in fact, is already happening to some degree as a result of the shortage of nurses, is that we need to describe outcomes and costs in relationship to staff delivery systems. A variation on the theme of substitutive function is differentiated practice, which despite its various definitions, matches the skills needed with the task (i.e., the staff classification with the nature of the job or role).

The other research project we need is a study of *magnet nursing homes*. When the magnet hospitals study was published in 1986, it was interesting to note that it focused on "nurse satisfiers," and not on "patient satisfiers." I did not get a sense that quality of care was an important measure of excellence in the hospital study, although the authors of the study stated that the magnet hospitals enjoyed good reputations for care. The idea came to me that I could use my nursing home facility to conduct a magnet nursing home study. My operative definition of excellence went beyond mere survey criteria. While space precludes description of the criteria, suffice it to say that I drew on input from residents, families, and non-nursing staff for their opinions about evidence (to them) of quality of care.

THE LAST WORD

There is no last word on quality. I suggest that quality is an evolving historical phenomenon driven by social philosophy, resource costs, and research into normal aging. In other words, we need to answer the question: what do we want long-term care facilities to do? What are they there to provide? We may need to establish those definitions and expectations before we can arrive at a comfortable decision about the imperatives and constituents of quality.

Appendix

New Directions in Nursing Home Ethics

Bart Collopy, Phillip Boyle, and Bruce Jennings

It has been said that the moral heart of a society can be judged by how well it provides for those at the dawn of life, those in the shadows of life, and those in the twilight of life. Nursing homes are places of lengthening shadows at twilight. By and large they are the last refuge in our society's broader system—if such a tattered, patchwork arrangement of overlapping and conflicting programs can be called that—of social support and provision for the elderly, the frail, and those with chronic illness and disability.

Some would like to think that eventually nursing homes can be eliminated, so that it will not be necessary to "institutionalize" anyone in the twilight of life. In an aging society, with increasing pressure on families as support systems, and inevitable limits on what home care or community-based elder care can provide, this is a misguided hope. Our efforts should be directed not at the eventual elimination of nursing homes, but at their improvement. There are, unfortunately, many pervasive cultural obstacles to a positive view of nursing homes. There is also a great need for further conceptual work and clarification in the ethics of nursing home care before we can ask, in a more constructive and positive vein, not just what we don't want nursing homes to do and to be, but also what we do want and expect of them.

In 1988 The Hastings Center began a two-year project on Nursing Home Ethics with support from The Pew Memorial Trust. Additional support from the Francis L. and Edwin L. Cummings Memorial Fund has allowed us to develop educational materials on ethical issues for nursing home professionals. The report offered here grows out of the overall work of the Nursing Home Ethics project. Our aim has been to open up a set of questions and to give a direction for future reflection and research, not to propose definitive answers for the range of exquisitely difficult, heart-rending quandaries that arise on a daily basis in nursing home care.

Nursing homes are not lacking in regulation, guidance, or advice from the outside. Nor are the ethical responsibilities of health care givers and families completely undelineated. But regulation and social policy is often inconsistent and sometimes makes good care harder rather than easier to provide—in part because we have not, as a society, truly worked out a moral vision and a set of aspirations for what we want nursing homes to be. Moreover, the ethical concepts available to decisionmakers in long-term and nursing home care are often drawn from bioethics paradigms designed for the problems of hospital-based and acute care. It is important to explore how notions based on acute care, particularly individualistic conceptions of autonomy and interests, can be modified so that they resonate more fully with the predicaments of nursing home residents, caregivers, and family members. If we can facilitate discussion of these matters in the nursing home industry and in the broader community, and if we can help to place these questions more securely on the research agenda of the field of bioethics, this report will have served its purpose.

We are most grateful for the expert advice, guidance, and support we received from the members of the project research group, and others who took part in several meetings held during the last two years. Many of the project group members have prepared their own papers on various topics touched upon in the following pages. Our plan is to publish these studies as a part of a comprehensive volume on ethical issues in long-term care that draws on past Hastings Center work on chronic illness and home care. In addition, we have assembled an ethics resource packet for nursing homes, especially those forming ethics committees or those interested in offering an in-house educational program for staff.

We would like to thank The Pew Memorial Trust and the Cummings Memorial Fund for providing the financial support that made our project and this Special Supplement possible.

Nursing homes can be frightening and depressing places. They remind us of our own mortality and of the inevitable time when most of us will face the frailty, ailments, and incapacities of old age. At the same time, nursing homes are places of refuge and respite; essential places to which exhausted families turn when they can't manage at home and when adequate community support is unavailable or unavailing. For some residents, too, moving to a nursing home represents escape from the loneliness, isolation, and danger of a solitary house or apartment. It means return to a social setting and a community of care and concern. Nursing homes are places to go home from—and many do. They can also be—and are—places people go home to.

How can we best make sense of the deep ambivalence, even the antipathy, that so many in our society feel toward nursing homes? How can we articulate a positive and constructive vision of the nursing home as a community of caring and a habitat that facilitates and nurtures the good living of the end of a life? To answer these questions we believe it is necessary to rethink some of the most common assumptions and orientations now applied to nursing homes in the regulations we impose upon them and in the ethical standards we ask them to meet.

First, we need to rethink the concept of autonomy, so central to bioethics in recent years. In the nursing home setting, because of the kinds of physical and mental limitations most residents face and because of the social functioning of a nursing home as an institution, autonomy and dependency cannot be seen as opposites. Instead, they must be seen as intertwined facets of one's life and one's state of being. Similarly, autonomy and community must be made mutually compatible in a nursing home setting if we are to get a full and realistic moral purchase on how life is actually lived there.

Second, we need to consider the difficult problem of justifiable limitations on individual freedom of choice and the institutional management of behavior. Problems of this type simply come up differently and have a different feel about them in a nursing home setting than they do in the acute-care context, or in most other spheres of social life. And they come up every single day.

Finally, we need to reconsider the basic directions and purposes of our public and regulatory policies concerning nursing home care. There is a growing awareness that an exclusive focus on protection and adversarialism in nursing home regulation is sometimes self-defeating. The policies and the means of their enforcement can create such defensiveness and rigidity in nursing homes that what should be the common goal of everyone involved, namely, the well-being and care of individual residents, gets lost in the process.

HISTORICAL ROOTS

The history of the modern nursing home has harsh beginnings, dating back to the 19th century almshouses and poorhouses that sheltered the destitute elderly. These institutions were places of both asylum and detention, housing a diverse population of the poor, the chronically disabled, and the mentally ill. Mid-19th-century morality tended to see poverty and disability, even in old age, as signs of an undisciplined, improvident, even profligate life. The harshness of the poorhouse and the social stigma attached to it were intended, therefore, to be socially therapeutic, prompting citizens to be provident for their old age and to avoid, at all costs, the bleak harbor of public dependency.

Despite their punitive morality and grim physical conditions, poorhouses remained the primary institutions for the dependent elderly well into the 20th century. Even though, near the turn of the century, churches and benevolent associations began to sponsor private old age homes, the number of elderly seeking refuge in county or municipal poorhouses continued to rise. Between 1880 and 1920 the proportion of poorhouse residents who were elderly rose from 33 percent to 66 percent, and during this time the poorhouse acquired an added, xenophobic stigma as immigrant inmates increased. In Thomas Cole's words, "By the end of the century . . . the poorhouse had evolved into a dumping ground for the isolated aged and infirm, a place for the destitute pauper to die. Almshouse superintendents and staff generally assumed that the majority of the inmates were unworthy—that is, chronically and illegitimately dependent on the state."

In the early decades of this century, state mental hospitals seemed initially to be better alternatives to the poorhouse—at least for the mentally incapacitated elderly. But mental hospitals soon proved to be dubious, if not dire, settings for elderly who suffered from the various dementias associated with aging. (Decades later, the deinstitutionalization movement would face the daunting task of finding more appropriate care settings for the large numbers of elderly "inmates" who roamed the corridors of the state hospitals.)

The period of the Great Depression saw a massive increase in the numbers of dependent elderly and, at the same time, a major breakthrough in care for the elderly through Social Security and other legislation that powerfully shaped the emergence of the modern nursing home. Although the Social Security system did not directly fund institutional care, it did provide fiscal resources to the elderly, enabling them to escape public dependency and to become "consumers" of long-term care services—a development that led to the growth of "proprietary" or for-profit homes for the elderly. In addition, Social Security in its early years did not provide payments to the elderly in public institutions—an exclusion that contributed crucially and purposefully to the demise of the county poorhouse. In the postwar period, federal legislation supporting hospital construction was expanded to include voluntary (nonprofit) nursing homes and, in time, proprietary nursing homes as well. Beginning in 1950, government funding for nursing home care steadily increased, culminating finally in the 1965 Medicaid program, which now covers more than 40 percent of all nursing home costs. At the same time, the role of nursing homes was sharply defined by developments elsewhere in the health care system. As hospitals increasingly specialized in short-term, acute care, nursing homes were more clearly defined as places for long-term care, especially of the elderly. Through the late 1950s and 1960s the role of nursing homes was also shaped by the deinstitutionalization movement that resulted in the discharge of large numbers of the elderly from mental hospitals. The result was further definition of the nursing home as a specialized institution—in this case for the care of the elderly who suffered from dementia and who could not be cared for in the community.

By the 1960s, then, the nursing home had emerged as the clearly recognized institutional setting for long-term care of the elderly. Through the next two decades, however, there were constant revelations of scandal—substandard and negligent care, outright abuse of residents, and a wide range of fiscal malfeasance, from embezzlement of residents' assets and extortion of money from families, to vendor kickbacks and reimbursement and capital finance fraud. While stricter government scrutiny and regulation has done much in the last ten years to rectify these abuses, the negative image of nursing homes persists, fueled by examples of "worst case" care that continue to come to public attention. In terms of enduring cultural image, the nursing home industry (even this frequently used designation has a pejorative resonance) still carries the taint of earlier institutional forms—the poorhouse and the commitment of the "senile" elderly to mental hospitals.

Even on the positive side, the government funding that has flowed to nursing homes over the last 30 years has often carried the priorities and reflected the fiscal pressures of the acute-care system. This is particularly true in today's cost-contained health care system. Reimbursement to nursing homes has become increasingly tighter and tied to high-care patients. The resulting "medical model" that comes with reimbursement overshadows psychosocial definitions of care, pressing the nursing home to be more a hospital manqué than an institution trying to be a home. In short, the modern nursing home suffers not only the stigma of its institutional predecessors and past scandals, but the strain of existing on the margins of a massive, often alien, health care system. For the foreseeable future at least, this means a continuing struggle for the nursing home community to posit a more accurate, balanced, and autonomous definition of itself.

PRESENT-DAY NURSING HOMES AND THEIR RESIDENTS

At present there are over 19,000 nursing homes in the United States (approximately 75 percent of them proprietary, 20 percent nonprofit, and 5 percent government-operated). The annual cost per resident in these homes ranges from an *average* of $28,000 in the northeastern states to $20,000 in the south. About 51 percent of such costs is paid directly by the elderly and their families; Medicaid covers about 44 percent, Medicare less than 2 percent, private insurance about 1 percent, and other government sources the rest. The small amount of coverage from Medicare and private insurance means that nursing home care is now the largest single health care cost paid for "out-of-pocket" by the elderly who do not rely on Medicaid. Facing such catastrophic costs, about 90 percent of the single elderly deplete their financial resources within a year after entering a nursing home; 50 percent of elderly couples face such depletion six months after one of them enters a nursing home. It is at this point, after "spend-down" to poverty levels determined by the individual states, that the elderly become eligible for Medicaid coverage of nursing home costs.

The number of elderly navigating these fiscal straits is already significant: 2.3 million now reside in nursing homes during the course of a year. With the continued aging of our population, this number is projected to increase by 75 percent over the next 30 years. In quick, calculable terms, this means that one in four individuals surviving to age 65 can expect to spend at least some time in a nursing home. The amount of time will vary—from short, recuperative stays to residency that may be permanent, extending months or years to the death of the individual. These statistics indicate the significant likelihood of nursing home placement for many of us, and when we factor in the shifting, highly "fluid" quality of the institutions in which we will be placed, it is not difficult to see why the nursing home is such a fearful and perplexing prospect.

The age of elderly nursing home residents ranges from 65 to 100 and over. Average age has been increasing and is now about 84, reflecting over the last decade a steady aging of our population that will intensify well into the middle of the next century. In terms of health status, nursing home residents generally suffer significant functional impairment and therefore need help with one or more activities of daily living—or ADLs, as they are called. Impairments in vision, hearing, and speech are common among residents, as are cognitive impairments. Approximately 63 percent of nursing home residents are reported to suffer from loss of memory or disorientation; about 47 percent suffer from serious dementia or organic brain damage. In terms of social and demographic factors, the majority of nursing home residents are women (only

25 percent are male) and widowed or single. They are also poor—either upon admission or as a result of a postadmission spend-down of resources to meet the high cost of care.

CULTURAL IMAGE

The ethical status of nursing homes is deeply affected by their cultural image. To the understandable dismay of those who study nursing homes or serve on their staffs, the popular image of these homes is often highly resistant to the basic facts about the frail elderly and their care. For the culture at large, nursing homes still summon up notions of neglect and abandonment. They still bear the taint of their "poorhouse" past and the pre-Social Security image of the elderly as an impoverished, dependent, socially stricken group.

This negative image is reinforced by some deep-seated cultural values. For a society passionate about personal independence and self-sufficiency, nursing homes are too easily seen as habitations for diminishment and dependency. For a culture that prizes curative medicine and the dream of "youthful aging," nursing homes are places of intractable, therefore intolerable, frailty. For a culture with deep anti-institutional biases and often romanticized versions of "family" and the freedoms of "home," nursing homes are especially suspect. They are "total institutions" where personal freedom, privacy, and range of choice have little chance. It is no surprise, then, that our general cultural wisdom warns us to avoid the nursing homes at all costs.

This negative image is powerful not only for the elderly but also for families who face the pain and stigma of "institutionalizing" one of their members. Here the negative image of the nursing home is reinforced by cultural expectations that families should always take care of their frail elderly. Such expectations are based on spousal and filial obligations, on the special relationships and ties of family life, on the priority of private over public responsibility for the elderly. Beyond notions of *obligation*, deeper impetus for such care comes, of course, from shared lives and burdens, from familial concern for the autonomy, dignity, and happiness of its elderly members, from a sense that the dependencies of frailty, like those of childhood, are best sheltered and supported in the "close" of the family.

But the cultural expectations nurtured by these values can produce a kind of moral aversion to nursing homes as places for "putting away" an elderly family member. Thus, nursing home admission is equated with familial abandonment, and the relatively full rosters of most nursing homes is proof of yet another breakdown of the family in the United States. Despite numerous studies that point to heavy care of the elderly as the *norm* in family relationships, the fiction persists that families continue, in large numbers, to "abandon" their elderly to nursing homes.

Here the gap between social reality and cultural image yawns wide. Family abandonment of the elderly is simply not the primary pattern in the United States. The typical nursing home placement is one in which family members painfully seek institutional care because their own care-giving capacities are inadequate or exhausted. Most families find themselves backed against the wall of last or only resort when they approach a nursing home. In fact, the burdens borne by families, the guilt and confusion sown into their lives by nursing home placement, indicate that the primary moral issue is not one of abandonment but the morally more perplexing one of determining the limits of family obligation to care for the elderly.

As long as the myth of family abandonment endures, however, nursing homes will be seen as places of dereliction. Moral pessimism about such care will remain deep seated, and avoiding the nursing home will continue to be the controlling, often uncritical, dictum for the elderly and their families. Unfortunately, such pessimism meshes all too smoothly with fiscal policies designed to keep the elderly out of nursing homes primarily for cost-containment reasons. It also reinforces the ageist bias that sees disability in later life as decimation and sad dénouement. From such a perspective, minimalist goals are enough. Keeping the elderly out of nursing homes is sufficient—despite the lessons we might have learned from experiments in deinstitutionalizing the mentally ill.

Eliminating inappropriate institutionalization of the elderly, especially in the face of mounting health care costs, is surely a morally, socially, and fiscally defensible goal, but if nursing homes are subjected to a general principle of avoidance they are doomed to be places of limited, if not parched, possibility. If nursing homes are seen only as a last, lamentable resort for the care of the elderly, then they will in effect be the Bedlams of our aging society, however technologized and overregulated we make them. There will be little enthusiasm in the public mind or in the mills of policy to define the "good institution," to recognize what human ends and needs the nursing home irreplaceably serves. Neither as individuals nor as a society will we develop a positive consensus about when and for whom nursing home care is really the best option, or how, for some individuals, institutional care can best sustain the last of life. Instead we will struggle to avoid these institutions, continue to fund them publicly only for the impoverished, and regulate them adversarially—because we have declared them essentially places of incapacity and abandonment. Those who live and work in nursing homes may know the reality of the good institution, but their experience runs against the grain of the cultural image and against the dominant priorities of the health care system.

THE PERPLEXITIES OF NURSING HOME ACCESS AND PLACEMENT

Confronting decisions about institutional care, the elderly and their families must contend not only with our culture's near taboo against nursing homes, but also with the pressures and complexities of the health care system. Over the last five years, Medicare's prospective payment system has effectively shortened the hospital stay for elderly patients. While this has led to cost savings in acute care, it has done so through "quicker and sicker" hospital discharges of the elderly. As a consequence, pressures have intensified on hospitals, as well as on the elderly and their families, to find adequate, often high-level, long-term care. In many areas of the country the number of nursing home beds has not kept pace with the growth of the elderly population. Moreover, Medicare and Medicaid coverage of formal home care services is tightly rationed; private payment for these services can be prohibitively expensive; and many families exhaust their own fiscal and other resources attempting to provide care themselves.

These systemic pressures drive the elderly and their families, as well as their care providers, into placement decisions that are short on time and options. In hospitals, decisions about nursing home care can be hurried—and harried—as Medicare's DRG clock runs down on a particular patient. In home care, family caregivers can find themselves at the brink of a placement decision because their elderly family member suddenly needs a higher level of care or because their own capacities to provide care have reached an inevitable, though perhaps long denied, point of burnout. Time is, of course, not the only restricting factor in such decisions. The health care system, operating with limited resources and deeply biased toward acute-care priorities, does not provide a solid continuum of care. It cannot offer a variety of institutional settings for chronic care plus a full range of community-based care services.

In the absence of this continuum many elderly have few options when they face the imperative of hospital discharge or when they find that the care available at home is no longer adequate. The number of nursing home beds is tightly limited, and access to these beds is further restricted by the specific level of care and the specific modes of payment and reimbursement to which they are tied. As a result, for all but the wealthiest elderly, a placement decision means facing the bureaucratic entanglements of Medicare and Medicaid coverage: confusing eligibility and copayment requirements, varied patterns of coverage, the difficulty of matching one's needs to the availability of a "Medicare bed" or a "Medicaid bed," complex rules about spend-down of fiscal resources as a requirement for coverage, and other requirements that can make nursing home admission a warren of confusion.

Under these pressures the "choice" of a nursing home is often far less than an autonomous weighing of options. In many instances, choosing a home comes down to *finding* one in what is distinctly a seller's market. Placement under such conditions turns what is in any case a difficult decision into a moral straitjacket. In desperation at finding any placement, elderly individuals can, in fact, find themselves signing admission agreements that restrict their rights to make health care decisions, to exercise autonomy in their daily living and financial arrangements, or to be informed of basic state and federal statutes regulating their care.

Over all of these difficulties falls another shadow—the fear of impoverishment. For any prolonged nursing home stay it is likely that

Medicare's relatively limited coverage will run out, that the elderly individual's own resources will be diminished, perhaps wholly swallowed by the high cost of nursing home care. The need of care that induces penury is one of the most fearsome aspects of nursing home placement for the elderly. It is also one of the most caustic social elements in our health care system. Despite constant calls for full, system-based attention, our health care policy continues only to tinker and make partial adjustments in long-term care, often with the goal of shifting costs to private parties and lessening the pressures on state budgets. As a result, Medicare coverage of nursing home care remains highly rationed. Medicaid coverage varies considerably from state to state and generally provides lower per capita payment to nursing homes than Medicare. This prompts homes to admit residents on the basis of the case mix most profitable to the home, and perhaps encourages a lower level of care for Medicaid residents. It is worth noting again that Medicaid assists many of the elderly only after their financial resources have been spent down and they have joined the ranks of the poor—a devastating route to public beneficence.

The distributive justice issues raised by the spend-down requirement demand analysis far beyond the scope of this discussion. In terms of the issue at hand it can be suggested, however, that existing health care policy reinforces the bleak image of the nursing home. For many of the elderly and their families, emotional antipathy to institutionalization is heightened by pressures of time, limited options, the complexity of the system to be negotiated, and the economic toll that nursing home care will levy.

The system also produces moral perplexity and conflict for providers of nursing home care. Achieving a suitable case mix of private-pay, Medicare, and Medicaid residents is crucial to the fiscal stability of most nursing homes. But that means accepting residents with a sharp eye to their sources of payment. Private paying residents generally pay higher fees, thus subsidizing Medicare and Medicaid residents and raising questions about equity and about "tiers" of care within homes. In addition, Medicare and Medicaid reimbursement rates clearly reflect acute-care priorities. With "quicker and sicker" discharges of the elderly from hospitals, nursing homes are pressed to provide higher and higher levels of care—and reimbursement rates favor these levels of care. Residents needing high-tech, skilled, or heavy-duty nursing care bring higher reimbursement than residents needing "custodial" care. This serves as an inducement for homes to accept the large numbers of high-care patients discharged by hospitals under the constraints of the DRG system. As the flow of such patients increases, hospital-like care is becoming increasingly standard in many nursing homes. There is less and less incentive for homes to care for those who were once familiar clients: elderly who may be very frail and unable to manage on their own in the community, but who are not acutely ill.

A large policy issue hides here, one that affects the basic mission of nursing homes and the very definition of institutional care of the frail elderly. Cost containment policies in acute care could in fact transform nursing homes into "subacute care" institutions. If the present pattern of escalating care continues, it is quite possible that nursing homes will, in the future, offer very little "intermediate" and domiciliary care. In short, they will be transformed from long-term care *homes* into long-term care *hospitals*. This would, of course, further erode the already thin continuum of care between hospital care and home care, leaving the health care system with few institutions providing assistance in daily living rather than high-level medical and nursing care. Deinstitutionalizing care to this extent would drastically narrow the mission of nursing homes. It would also massively increase the burdens on families, many of whom would have very limited access to formal home care services. Such reduction of institutional care, while it might produce fiscal savings in the health care system, would also bring disheartening social costs.

"BEING A RESIDENT":
THE CONSTRAINTS OF THE INSTITUTION

The difficulties of access and admission to a nursing home can foreshadow the more persistent problems that individuals face once they become residents. For many elderly, admission to a nursing home is quite definitely a "placement"—to use the impersonal and passive, but quite common phrase. Placement stands as a clear marker of dependency, a late-life rite of passage announcing loss of capacity and control.

Moreover, even for individuals who may have actively participated in the placement process, institutionalization can seem a death blow to autonomy. Even when a nursing home stay is relatively short, it can be a dark omen of what lies ahead as one continues to age. For those who face long-term institutionalization, who see the nursing home as life's last domicile, admission may signal separation, isolation, and rejection; it may summon up images of loss, of a stripped and even mutilated self.

The very terminology of the nursing home offers some clues to these images. Being a "resident" in a nursing "home" is quite different from being a patient in a hospital. Despite the domestic descriptors, "residency" can prove more fully and finally disruptive than hospitalization. Admission to a nursing home separates one, sometimes permanently, from the personal and social contexts of one's previous life. *This* home can seem an alien place, filled with the frail and incapacitated, where one's past has no roots or recognition, where one must join others, mostly strangers, in attempting to live a private life in a public place. At its worst *this* home is thick with contiguity but thin in community. Here, personal choice and social ambit shrink in the midst of unchosen others, in dependency on caregivers whose authority governs even the minutiae of daily life.

The potentially invasive and disenfranchising impact of the nursing home is perhaps best summed up in Erving Goffman's classic account of the "total institution." Total institutions are characterized by their all-encompassing, highly controlled settings and their pervasive authority structure. Daily life in a total institution is tightly scheduled and is organized around "batch processing" of inmates or residents. Managing the daily lives of a large number of persons in a relatively small space with limited resources leads, almost inescapably, to surveillance and control of behavior, hierarchical staff-inmate interaction, and the dominance of routines that serve the institution's efficiency. In its closeting and control of the individual, the total institution acts, finally, as a barrier to the outside world and the previous identities and life activities of its inhabitants.

A simple categorization of nursing homes as irredeemably "total" institutions would be facile and inaccurate. On the other hand, the model of the total institution can be analytically useful. It offers a stark indictment of the poor nursing home and a sharp, if negative, template for the good nursing home. Accordingly, the good home would be one that resists institutional constraint and control, that works against the collectivization of residents, that checks the primacy of the institutional agenda over the interests of residents. In terms of fundamental ethical categories, this would mean a commitment not only to the good care and safety of residents but also to their autonomy, independence, and dignity. At the same time, the good nursing home must respond to counterbalancing values: the common good, the mutual responsibilities of residents, the requirements of equity and justice, the prudential use of limited resources, the obligations imposed by legal and regulatory requirements.

TOWARD AUTONOMY WITHIN COMMUNITY

If DRGs, Medicare, and public policy in general have tended to press nursing homes in the direction of acute care, so too, in its own way, has bioethics. Like public policy, most prevailing ethical perspectives have made the mistake of regarding nursing home care as an extension of hospital care. Like public policy, bioethics has failed to understand that nursing homes can be communities where ongoing managed care is given to some of the most frail, dependent, and vulnerable members of our moral community.

If we are to reorient our society's understanding of nursing homes with a view to changing our behavior, we must first appreciate some of the implications of our most commonsensical ethical assumptions regarding institutionalized long-term care. By exploring some of the ways in which the standard assumptions of bioethics fall short, we can lay the groundwork for a more adequate ethical perspective.

The central figure of the standard bioethical analysis is the competent adult, ill enough to seek medical assistance and to that extent vulnerable, but still essentially at the height of his or her powers. The moral personhood of the individual, the property with which bioethics is most concerned, is not undermined or transformed by illness; it stands apart from the physical condition of the patient. This view rests on an understanding of the body as essentially a container for the self—an animate, dynamic, amazingly complex and wondrous container, to be sure, but a container nonetheless. An individual, virtually paralyzed and physically dependent on total life support, remains no less a moral person for all that.

More surprisingly, moral personhood is in some ways independent of the mind as well. For we say that an individual who is permanently unconscious remains a person in the moral sense; the individual's rights and protections remain unaffected by the destruction of the brain and loss of the mind, even though the capacity to exercise those rights directly and without assistance has been lost. Thus bioethics places great emphasis on advance directives, thinking that the record of the past voice of the incompetent patient is the best way to respect the moral personhood that still exists before us in the unconscious or demented individual.

In a very real and literal sense, then, the intact moral personhood of the patient presides over the entire ethical analysis of how health professionals and representatives of society—administrators, lawyers, and public officials—should treat that patient. As a moral person the patient bears rights, liberties, and interests that place strong moral (and sometimes also legal) obligations on others to act or to forbear from action as this affects the patient. The values and principles that bioethical analysis relies upon are notions such as rights, liberties, self-determination or autonomy, privacy, doing good (beneficence), not doing harm (nonmaleficence), and justice. These values and principles have different meanings and different implications for the right conduct of others. They often conflict, or at least cannot all be honored to the same degree simultaneously, and so must be balanced. Nonetheless, for all their differences, these various bioethical concepts have a common notion at their core: they are largely designed to ensure the moral person sufficient resources, assistance, and freedom from interference to allow him to be a rationally self-directing being. Bioethics seeks to carve out—even in the face of sickness, curtailment of function, and dependency—the moral space needed for a human being to live life in his or her own way.

Two things make this picture of moral personhood and its protection an especially compelling one in bioethics. For one thing, its individualistic assumptions are deeply embedded in American culture. For another, these individualistic assumptions are no less deeply ingrained in the concept of acute care. In acute-care medicine the disease state that medical help is to combat can be seen as a condition thoroughly external to the moral personality of the patient. Disease is a threat that renders the restrictive environment of the hospital setting tolerable—but only to the extent that it furthers the patient's goal of cure and freedom from the disease threat. The acute-care setting is by its very nature and purpose a temporary imposition and restriction on freedom.

This makes it reasonable to view the medical setting in thoroughly instrumental terms. Hospitals have no value whatsoever apart from their contribution to the enterprise of healing, at least not from the perspective of the ordinary patient. They are not places we seek out and choose to stay in if we do not have to; they are unpleasant and even dangerous places, to be avoided by the well.

In its advocacy for the moral person of the patient, bioethics constantly monitors and scrutinizes the medical setting, including the behavior of the physicians and other health care providers who act to limit the patient's freedom. The objective of this monitoring is to see to it that the setting imposes only those restrictions necessary to achieve the ends of the treatment plan, and to ensure that the interests of the patient, and not the interests of the caregivers or the caregiving institution, come first. Bioethical analysis can defend the patient's moral person by arguing that medical decisionmaking should be guided as much as possible by a respect for the autonomy of the patient, so that, in effect, the patient can monitor his or her own care and can legitimize restrictions on his or her liberty by consenting to them. When the patient is not competent, and when his or her wishes are not known and cannot be reasonably inferred from advance directives, then the patient-centered orientation demands that treatment decisions be made in the "best interests" of the patient, accommodating the interests of others when possible, but overriding them in all cases where there is irremediable conflict.

Our point here is not to reject the advocacy of the moral person, nor to deny its very significant contribution to the protection and wellbeing of individual patients—to say nothing of its contribution to medicine as an ethical, healing enterprise. But serious problems arise when this framework and its underlying assumptions are carried over without qualification into the realm of nursing home care.

No one who has followed discussions of residents' rights in nursing homes in recent years can doubt that the ethics of acute care have been carried over into the nursing home. Almost without exception these discussions have been dedicated to the protection of the autonomous moral personhood of the resident—a personhood seen as undiminished and fully worthy of continuing respect despite the infirmities and loss of function that brought the patient to the nursing home in the first place. And since the dominant orientation is protection and respect of that autonomous personhood, it follows that bioethics should bring to the nursing home setting the same attitude of monitoring it brought to the hospital setting.

We believe that our understanding of the ethical dilemmas faced by caregivers, nursing home residents, and their families would be improved by a conception of autonomy rooted within community. In contrast to the highly individualistic conception of autonomy now prevalent in acute-care ethics, "autonomy within community," as we shall call it, draws on a notion of moral personhood that is not abstracted from the individual's social context or state of physical and mental capacity.

If nursing homes are seen primarily as institutions of support for persons whose aging or chronic illness has reduced their independence and created special needs, then caregiving can no longer be seen as merely a service or external intervention that either threatens or serves the person's interests. For now the caring constitutes the fabric of the person's life. The person depends on that fabric of support, and the reality of the moral situation is that the person must embrace dependency rather than resisting it as a temporary, external threat. Nursing homes must be founded on the realization, so difficult to achieve in American culture, that dependency has a positive and proper place in the scheme of human life. In certain situations of incapacity, autonomy and respect for persons simply come to mean the creative, enabling use of dependency to give richer meaning to the lives of individuals who can no longer be self-reliant.

We believe that a new agenda for the ethics of long-term nursing home care could be set by seeing nursing homes as communities of caring and interdependency. The goal should be not simply to eliminate or minimize dependency whenever possible, but to make a genuinely creative and nurturing use of the dependency that is an inevitable reality for most nursing home residents. Nursing homes are rarely places of curing, but they can and should be places of healing—of making whole—of enabling frail or chronically ill persons to use their dependency to grow as human beings.

ETHICS OF COMMUNITY

When we apply this new perspective to the daily details of nursing home life we become sensitive to the often unnoticed, routine blocking, the barely discernible "clotting," of autonomy that takes place in a nursing home. Instead of the typical informed consent "event" or "discrete decision" scenario, the nursing home more often presents a diffuse, ongoing, incremental flow of acceptance and refusal, acquiescence and noncooperation, negotiation and trial. The most characteristic dilemma a nursing home resident faces is not a life-or-death decision, but the pervasive lack of personal control that starts at the door with the traumatic admission and permeates a resident's daily life, ranging from dressing oneself, to eating, to doing what one wants when one wants.

A painful area of broad conflict, routine in long-term care but relatively rare in acute care, is dangerous and disruptive behavior. The close, communal living of the nursing home, complicated by a high incidence of physical frailty and dementia among residents, leads to difficult questions about the control or management of resident behavior. Nursing home staff have a responsibility to protect the safety of all residents, the privacy of their places and persons, the basic order and social amenity of their collective life. This can require a corrective response to the resident who wanders aimlessly and intrusively, who is physically or verbally abusive, or who otherwise pushes beyond the limits of what the group is able to tolerate. Yet staff equally have a responsibility to use the most benign means possible to control or modify residents' behavior. Rigid notions of safety and good order can lead to overly invasive interventions—the most questionable of which, as we indicate later, is the widespread use of physical or pharmacological restraints.

MORAL ECOLOGY: THE INSTITUTION

Nursing homes possess a moral ecology quite different from the ecology of acute care. The setting—the nursing home itself as an institution with its routines and programs, peopled by its residents, family, and staff—makes all the moral difference. In hidden ways, environmental factors subvert autonomy, both individual and communal. The coercive power of the institution where one lives can be more subtle and pervasive than that of the hospital where one only "stays."

The environment necessarily encroaches on individual liberties as one attempts to live a private life in a public institution. Living quarters sometimes amount to a shared bedroom with only a few feet around a bed to call one's own, and no ultimate say over who occupies the next bed. Privacy and space are at a minimum. Insufficient storage areas may require limiting one's possessions, yet the security of even these few personal items cannot be assured.

Public areas are no better. Noise levels rise in common areas as people try to accommodate those with impaired hearing or to override repetitive moans or other din created by confused residents. Compounding these problems, daily life in a nursing home is driven by routines: fixed times for baths, meals, medication, getting up, and going to bed. The nursing home's restriction of personal privacy and freedom is fueled by communal need for operational efficiency and the obligation to foster the ongoing, total well-being of the individual. When it is fueled by external pressures, such as fear of litigation or regulatory penalty, restriction of freedom is more dubious.

When caregivers and residents have long-term relationships that reach beyond medical care into the activities of daily life, the ramifications of refusal and noncompliance are more complex than they are in acute care. Habitual noncompliance or refusal of care may be more a residents' revolt against the institutional environment than a considered judgment about a particular aspect of a care plan. As the staff become more intimately acquainted with each resident and learn to decipher refusal and noncompliance in the light of residents' personal histories, a new concept of autonomy—autonomy within community—can improve the institutional environment and enhance the quality of the patient's life.

MORAL ECOLOGY: RESIDENTS AS
MORAL AGENTS

Too many nursing home residents, functionally impaired, watch in dismay as slowly but surely the physical self-reliance they have always taken for granted evaporates. Residents need more help with one or more basic activities of daily living, such as dressing, grooming themselves, bathing, getting to the toilet, and getting in and out of bed. Control over the little things of life—what to wear, what and when to eat—vanishes.

In addition, where there is cognitive impairment, this diminishes residents' decisional capacity, making even more devastating inroads on their autonomy. In long-term care, much more so than in acute care, questions of mental capacity shape decisions about medical treatment, about the rights of idiosyncratic choice and behavior, about an individual's authority to make even commonplace decisions. The reported incidence of dementia among elderly nursing home residents is far higher than among the general hospital population, but these reports can be read in two ways. On the one hand, they can be useful in guarding residents against potential harm, as they caution staff not to make unwarranted assumptions about a resident's good judgment. On the other hand, reports of high incidence of mental incapacity can foster blanket assumptions that elderly nursing home residents are "generally" or "typically" incapacitated—and that their autonomy should usually yield to the beneficence of caregivers.

Decisional incapacity is, in principle, a warrant for overriding a patient's wishes and for vesting others with surrogate responsibility. For this reason, assessments of mental competence carry massive moral weight. But decisional incapacity is not always a clear matter. Nursing home residents may, for example, experience fluctuating or intermittent competence, a condition that requires careful interpretation and a response that respects choices made in periods of clarity. Similarly, residents may suffer from mental confusion and incapacity that is quite reversible and results from physical or emotional trauma, overmedication, or metabolic imbalance. Cases of this sort sometimes require elaborate monitoring or titration of medication, but these strategies are not standard practice in every nursing home.

Since assessments of incapacity limit the moral agency of residents and effectively disenfranchise them in the decision-making process, it is especially crucial that these assessments not be global, but instead focus on capacity for specific decisions and responsibilities. The resident who cannot manage her finances might be able to decide about major surgery or whom she wants as a roommate. The resident who is visually and aurally impaired might be clear in his thinking, even though he cannot execute his wishes and perhaps has great difficulty even communicating them.

The position taken some years ago by the President's Commission for the Study of Ethical Problems in Medicine and Biomedical and Behavioral Research, that decisional capacity can be determined by an informed layperson's judgments, is especially helpful for long-term care. If assessments of decisional capacity are understood as nonmedical rather than clinical, then their moral nature becomes clear. The assessment of incapacity is the judgment that a nursing home resident is unable to function as an independent moral agent in a specific area of choice and behavior. As determination of incapacity will place at risk significant interests of the resident, there is a real need for cautious, carefully limited, regularly reviewed assessments. Such an approach would be a check against quick "diagnoses" of incapacity based on mental status tests that provide only an initial screening of mental functioning and do not resolve complex questions about the extent or specificity of an individual's capacity. In some cases, neurologic or psychiatric evaluation alone can provide clear assessments of capacity, but the most difficult assessments may require first-hand experience of a resident's decisional style and value preferences, an ongoing relationship that the resident is more likely to have with his daily caregivers than with the specialist called in to make a clinical diagnosis.

MORAL ECOLOGY: FAMILY AND STAFF AS MORAL AGENTS

The involvement of family members in decisionmaking is also more extensive, and takes place over a longer period of time in nursing home care than in acute care. Thus family members can provide substantial help in enhancing the autonomy of a nursing home resident, as well as mediating situations of conflict or difficult communication. But family members can also be overbearing. Sometimes families function as a kind of extended client, to the point that the resident's interests and preferences are submerged by the family's wishes. In more extreme cases, families may step in and simply take control away from the resident. The family's needs and involvement are therefore crucial but clearly complicating factors in long-term care. Sorting out the questions of how many people's wishes must be honored, and whose wishes have priority, is vitally important in long-term care. Just who the client is, and thus to whom obligations are owed, is not always clear in communities defined by ongoing mutual need and interdependence.

The round-the-clock care staff typically provide is not performed chiefly by registered nurses but by a paraprofessional pool that makes up the bulk of the workforce within nursing homes. This paraprofessional workforce—poorly paid, minimally trained, and overworked—confronts the prospect of an evening or night shift with a patient load of 50 to 100 residents. The staff's vision of what kind of place nursing homes ought to be is often blocked by the demands of routine and the pressures of short staffing. Too little time is available for creative problem solving. Too little institutional support is available to help staff maintain a careful balance between serving the common good of a vulnerable, dependent population and respecting the dignity of each resident.

VULNERABILITY AND RESTRAINT

The moral atmosphere of nursing homes is palpable to anyone who enters one: residents are strapped to wheelchairs by Posey vests, or tethered to beds with soft wrist and ankle restraints, and sometimes with four-point leather straps. The rationale is, of course, that restraints are employed for the residents' own good. The resident's own safety might prompt the use of restraints, as frailty, poor balance, and unattended wandering can lead to physical injury. Frequently, staff employ devices to restrain residents from striking out at other residents. More disturbingly, however, restraints may be used because of institutional fear of litigation, the ready availability of the devices, insufficient staffing, and staff attitudes.

Use of restraints is not infrequent: a 1991 JAMA survey found that as many as 59 percent of patients in nursing homes were in restraints, a percentage almost double that of restrained patients in acute care. In a high percentage of cases of physical restraint, physicians give no written orders approving restraints. Any restriction of movement demands a strong justification. In a free society there is not only a presumption in favor of freedom; there is a further presumption that the burden of proving the need to curtail freedom falls on the party doing the restraining.

The use of physical restraints must be roundly challenged—and the tide is now turning, although it may be washing out some important concerns about the welfare of the community as a whole. Ample evidence indicates physical restraints are generally inappropriate. No one sanctions the rare instances in which restraints are used to punish residents for refusing to obey staff orders. Nor, in the light of medical evidence, can we defend the more frequent use of restraints to protect residents from hurting themselves. Far from protecting patients from harm, restraints inflict it. Physical risks include bed sores, infections, reduced circulation, muscle weakness, pneumonia, loss of appetite, and incontinence caused by immobility, to name but a few. Worse yet, instances in which residents are found hanging dead from the bedrail, strangled by the restraint, are increasingly coming to light. Psychological risks, more difficult to quantify, include humiliation, fear of abandonment, impairment of self-image, agitation, panic, and disorientation.

Common concerns about the legal need to restrain are inflated. Legal liability is based on whether due care was exercised under the circumstances, not simply on whether a resident was injured. In fact, the legal literature suggests that no institution has been successfully sued simply for failure to protect residents. There is no duty to restrain. Misplaced perception of liability overlooks the fact that a growing number of plaintiffs have sued successfully over the misapplication of restraints.

Questions of effectiveness aside, the use of restraints is open to the criticism that it is practiced on a vulnerable population ripe for abuse.

Nursing home residents are sensorially impaired; their dwindling vision, hearing, and speech impedes ability meaningfully to perceive risk or understand the staff's concerns. Likewise, they are less likely to have the ability to communicate objections to being restrained. As if their physical and sometimes mental vulnerability were not enough, nursing home residents are also socially vulnerable. The majority are women, and many are of low socioeconomic standing. In a context of clear power differentials such as gender and class, the use of restraints is even more objectionable.

Critics of restraints assume (correctly, we believe) that our moral obligations entail fostering an environment that helps people to flourish, despite their frailty and illness. To this end, they have provided viable alternatives to the routine use of physical restraints. Alternatives call for an understanding of why residents fall or strike others. Remedies in some cases require reeducating or providing sensory stimulation to adapt confused patients to their environment. The environment can also be adjusted by determining what makes residents want to move, such as drafts or noise. Devices that enhance mobility (including walkers, braces, eyeglasses, and hearing aids) and devices that lessen injury (such as low adjustable beds) must be considered. Providing for the least restrictive environment in some cases means creatively reshaping the environment—recruiting volunteer sitters, or erecting visual barriers such as bright lines at door thresholds.

The practical and moral creativity of finding alternatives to restraints might lull caregivers into supposing that autonomy within the community has been adequately provided for. Those who suggest alternatives to restraints tend to overlook the related, but broader problems of behavior management that cannot be reshaped quite so easily. Residents often wonder when they can go for a walk, or why times for their rising and sleeping are regulated, or why they can't wash their clothes in their sink. External regulations of mundane daily activities, together with the coaxing, badgering, pleading, and other manipulation that is involved in getting residents to take medications or baths challenges any institution to respond creatively to the dependency of its residents.

Physical restraints are at one end of a continuum of behavior management, the other end being the informal and humane manipulation that all people experience. Nursing homes manage behavior inappropriately not only when they use force, but also when they use coercive pressures and schedules, and when they fail to provide at least a minimal range of choices, options, and opportunities for residents. Sometimes the means of control used are patently offensive to human dignity—for example, language and behavior that infantilizes residents. Less blatant are the subtle rewards given for cooperating with the staff and the administration, through informal identification of "good" residents and perhaps through visits from administrators themselves. It may well be these imperceptible and mundane issues that most challenge the mainstream model of autonomy, because they make us refine moral obligations in the light of communal living.

As we suggested earlier, an individualistic interpretation of autonomy yields a bioethics that provides safeguards from encroachments on all liberty. Such a view leaves nursing home staff wondering how to fulfill obligations for the caring necessary for each resident to flourish, no matter how diminished his or her functional or mental capacity. No one objects to the daily multitude of ways that we convince and cajole others to do what we want, as long as it leaves them meaningful choices. Further, everyone agrees that communal life does not support a notion that "man's home is his castle." Autonomy within community entails a certain whittling away of maximal liberties, which may or may not be justified depending on the community in question.

Such justification can only be given in light of the kinds of places we think nursing homes ought to be. Despite the too-prevalent tendency to see nursing homes as subacute care centers, they are homes. Too often we forget—or deny—that nursing homes are places to *live*. Our homes optimally supply an environment for human flourishing, no matter what disabilities afflict us. In home life, assertions of an individual's autonomy give way, not because of mere subterfuge, but because home life provides a set of goods that cannot be gotten if each resident is completely autonomous. Affirmation of personal worth in spite of physical or mental frailty; a sense of belonging; the assurance that the resident may trust others in the community to safeguard person and dignity; the value of interdependence and connection that keeps us all from isolation; the concern for others that translates into practical acts of care for the body—these goods of community are available to its members only if they affirm each other and the common good.

THE PARADOX OF REGULATION

Nursing homes today are surrounded by stigma, suspicion, and mistrust. The development of the nursing home industry and all too frequent scandals involving the most shocking kinds of abuse and neglect have inevitably reinforced the negative image of nursing homes. In addition, whether rightly or wrongly, many families feel guilt when they place a frail elder in a nursing home, as if they had abandoned the person or somehow failed to live up to their moral responsibilities. As guilt is a powerful emotion, and as nursing homes have earned some of the mistrust they suffer, it should surprise no one that they are subject to closer governmental scrutiny and more detailed regulation than other health care institutions. In the eyes of many, progressive reform in long-term care requires even broader regulation, with stricter oversight and tougher enforcement. We wonder about that.

There can be no question that there is serious and continuing need for strict regulation, oversight, and accountability. The rights of residents and their families must be protected, high standards must be maintained, and abuses must be detected, punished, and prevented from happening again. Yet at some point, overregulation itself becomes an obstacle to the very objectives it seeks to attain.

The question we would like to pose is what moral approach to take to the problem of nursing home regulation. Will individualistic notions of autonomy and personhood and the associated ethic of protection yield the most insight? Or does this way of thinking about the purpose of regulation in long-term care lead to the same sorts of confusion we encountered earlier?

In general, nursing home regulation is a matter of striking a delicate balance between that degree of control necessary to insure a basic standard of decent and humane care, and that degree of professional discretion needed to allow nursing homes to respond to their own particular problems of care as they make creative use of the dependency that is an essential fact of nursing home life. The balance is particularly difficult to strike when, as happens often, the administration and staff of nursing homes react to regulations in a defensive and self-protective way, looking more to the letter than the spirit of the law, and responding with inflexible procedures that satisfy the regulations but do not fully address residents' needs. Certainly, the blame for this state of affairs cannot be placed solely on the shoulders of nursing home professionals. In many places the attitude of regulators is so adversarial, and the use of administrative threats so heavy-handed, that creative problem solving and cooperation between nursing home professionals and government regulators is virtually impossible.

Can this vicious circle of mistrust and defensiveness be broken? Probably not easily or soon. We believe, however, that a modest beginning can be made if we could shift our understanding of the nature and goals of regulation in the area of long-term care. Because we have not fully developed the proper model for thinking about the kind of place that a nursing home is and should be—it is neither a hospital nor an apartment building—we remain uncertain as to what practical goals should guide regulatory standards and the evaluations that are conducted during nursing home surveys. We are, however, convinced that the perspective must shift from an ethic of protection to an ethic of the creative use of dependency within communities of caring.

As we think about the purpose of regulation, we need to move away from an emphasis on its negative function as a sanctioning, threatening mechanism for extorting acceptable conduct, and toward a more positive view. Regulation should not begin with the premise that, if left to themselves, nursing home caregivers are naturally prone to abusive practices. Nor should it be seen either by regulators or by caregivers as snares and traps set to capture wrongdoers and people of ill will. Instead, regulation should be seen as a tool that allows professionals who are motivated to do the right thing to do their jobs better and more creatively than they otherwise could.

At a minimum, stepping out of the vicious circle of nursing home regulation will require two long strides. The first step involves education and creating conditions for a more positive dialogue between regulators and caregivers. The second step is to professionalize the nursing home industry and to raise it in society's esteem. Only through better training, more adequate compensation, and self-regulation—in short, the marks of professionalization—can nursing home care live down its current dubious reputation.

Finally, as new regulations are devised, we should experiment with a legislative approach that is less intrusive and detailed than what we have now. Policymakers and regulators should set broad guidelines for acceptable practice, as well as providing incentives for good and creative innovations in individual nursing homes. In turn, local administrators should be in much closer dialogue with regulators so that they can fashion specific practices that fit within those broader guidelines. In this approach, we as a society would put considerable discretion into the hands of nursing home professionals, and we would rely on the soundness of the governance mechanisms within specific nursing homes. We need to scrutinize these mechanisms too, to ensure that residents, family members, and the surrounding community are fully represented.

At the end of the day we will never find the imagination and the courage to experiment creatively with nursing home practices and policies until we embark on a far broader and more open public conversation about the positive side of what we want nursing homes to be. The trouble is that we cannot really talk about nursing homes without also examining the values and aspirations we hope to discover in ourselves in the twilight of our lives. Can we summon the courage to look into that twilight and find something to affirm there?

SELECTED REFERENCES

Achenbaum, W. A. (1978). *Old age in the new land*. Baltimore: Johns Hopkins University Press.

Ambrogi, D. M., & Leonard, F. (1988, June). The impact of nursing home admission agreements on resident autonomy. *The Gerontologist 28*, (supplement) 82–89.

Besdine, R. W. (1983). Decisions to withhold treatment from nursing home residents. *Journal of the American Geriatric Society, 31*,(10), 602–606.

Buehler, D. A. (1990). Informed consent and the elderly: An ethical challenge for critical care nursing. *Critical Care Nursing Clinics of North America, 2*(3), 461–471.

Callahan, D. (1985, Winter). Feeding the dying elderly. *Generations*, 15–17.

———. (1987). What do the young owe the old? In *Setting limits: Medical goals in an aging society*. New York: Simon and Schuster.

Cantor, M. H. (1983, December). Strain among caregivers: A study of experience in the United States. *The Gerontologist, 23*, 597–604.

Cohen, E. S. (1988, June). The elderly mystique: Constraints on the autonomy of the elderly with disabilities. *The Gerontologist, 28* (supplement), 10–17.

Cole, T. R. (1987, Summer). Class, culture, and coercion: An historical look at longterm care. *Generations, 11*, 9–15.

Collopy, B. (1988, June). Autonomy in long-term care: Some crucial distinctions. *The Gerontologist, 28* (supplement), 10–17.

Dubler, N., & Zuckerman, C., The ethics of home care: Autonomy and accommodation. *Hastings Center Report, 20,*(2).

Daniels, N. (1988). *Am I my parents' keeper?* New York: Oxford University Press.

Dunlop, B. B. (1979). *The growth of nursing home care.* Lexington, MA: D.C. Heath.

Dunn, H. (1990). *Hard choices for loving people: CPR, artificial feeding tubes and the nursing home resident.* Fairfax Nursing Center, 10701 Main Street, Fairfax, VA 22030.

Eustis, N., Greenberg, J., & Patten, S. (1984). *Long-term care for older persons: A policy perspective.* Monterey, CA: Brooks/Cole.

Fowler, M. D. (1989) Ethical decisionmaking in clinical practice. *Nursing Clinics of North America, 24,*(4), 955–965.

Glasser, G., Zweibel, N., & Cassel, C. (1988). The ethics committee in the nursing home: Results of a national survey. *Journal of the American Geriatric Society, 36,*(2), 150–156.

Goffman, E. (1961). *Asylums.* New York: Doubleday.

Grant, L. A. (1985). *The nursing home in American society.* Baltimore: Johns Hopkins.

High, Dallas, (1988, June). All in the family: Extended autonomy and exceptions in surrogate health care decisionmaking. *The Gerontologist, 28*, 46–51.

Institute of Medicine, Committee on Nursing Home Regulations, (1986). *Improving the quality of care in nursing homes.* Washington, D.C.: National Academy Press.

Jennings, B., Callahan, D., & Caplan, A. L. (1988). Ethical challenges of chronic illness. *Hastings Center Report, 19,*(2).

Johnson, C. L., & Grant, L. A. (1985). Institutionalization and its effects on the elderly. In *The nursing home in American society*. Baltimore: Johns Hopkins University Press.

Johnson, S. (1990, Fall). The fear of liability and the use of restraints in nursing homes. *Law, Medicine and Health Care, 18*(3), 263–273.

Kane, R. L., & Kane, R. A. (1989). *Long-term care: Principles, programs, and policies*. New York: Springer.

Kane, R. A., & Caplan, A. L. (Eds.) (1990). *Everyday ethics: Resolving dilemmas in nursing home life*. New York: Springer.

Kapp, M. B. (1987). Family decisionmaking for nursing home residents: Legal mechanisms and ethical underpinnings. *Theoretical Medicine, 8*, 259–273.

Kayser-Jones, Schmit, J. (1981). *Old, alone and neglected*. Berkeley and Los Angeles: University of California Press.

Keenan, M. P. (1989). *Changing needs for long-term care*. Washington, D.C.: Public Policy Institute, AARP.

Kilner, J. (1989, October). Age criteria in medicine: Are the medical justifications ethical? *Archives of Internal Medicine, 149*, 2343–2346.

LaPuma, J., & Moss, R. (1991). The ethics of mechanical restraints. *Hastings Center Report, 21*,(1), 22–25.

Lerner, M., & Rigert, J. (1990, December). Safeguards that kill. *Star Tribune*, 2–5.

Lidz, C. W. & Arnold, R. M. (1990). Institutional constraints on autonomy. *Generations, 14* (supplement), 65–68.

Lo, B., & Dornbrand, L. (1984). Sounding board: Guiding the hand that feeds. *New England Journal of Medicine, 311*(6), 402–404.

———. (1989, September). Understanding the benefits and burdens of tube feeding. *Archives of Internal Medicine, 149*, 1925–1926.

Lynn, J. (1986, June). Ethical issues in caring for elderly residents of nursing homes. *Primary Care, 13*(2), 295–306.

May, W., et al. (1987). Feeding and hydrating the permanently unconscious and other vulnerable persons. *Issues in Law & Medicine, 3*(3), 203–217.

McCarrick, P. M. (1988, June). Withholding or withdrawing nutrition or hydration. *Scope Note 7*. Kennedy Institute of Ethics, Georgetown University.

Meltzer, J., Farrow, F. & Richman, H. (Eds.). (1985). *Policy options in long-term care*. Chicago: University of Chicago Press.

Miles, S. H., et al. (1988). Nursing home policies addressing the use of withdrawal of life-sustaining medical treatments. *Clinics in Geriatric Medicine,* 4(3), 681–690.

Moody, H. R. (1988, June). From informed consent to negotiated consent. *The Gerontologist, 28* (supplement), 64–70.

Nelson, J. L. (1990, Spring). Paternalism and parenthood. *Journal of Social Philosophy, 21,* 107–118.

President's Commission for the Study of Ethical Problems in Medicine and Biomedical and Behavioral Research. (1982). Who is incapacitated and how is it to be determined? In *Making health care decisions.* Washington, D.C.: U.S. Government Printing Office.

Rango, N. (1985). The nursing home resident with dementia: Clinical care, ethics, and policy implications. *Annals of Internal Medicine, 102*(8), 835–841.

Rivlin, A. M., & Wiener, J. M. (1988). *Caring for the disabled elderly: Who will pay?* Washington, D.C.: The Brookings Institution.

Rose, S. R. (1988). *Uneasy endings: Daily life in an American nursing home.* Ithaca: Cornell University Press.

Shanas, E. (1979, April). The family as a social support system in old age. *The Gerontologist, 19,* 169–174.

Stephens, S. A., & Christianson, J. B. (1986). *Informal care of the elderly.* Lexington, MA: Lexington Books.

Stone, R., Cafferata, G. L., & Sangl, J. (1987). Caregivers of the frail elderly: A national profile. *The Gerontologist, 27,* 616–626.

Tancredi, L. R. (1987, Summer). The mental status examination. *Generations, 11,* 24–31.

Tinetti, M. E., et al. (1991, January). Mechanical restraint use among residents of skilled nursing facilities: Prevalence, patterns, and predictors. *Journal of the American Medical Association, 265,* 468–471.

Tobin, S. S., & Lieberman, M. A. (1976). *Last home for the aged.* San Francisco: Jossey-Bass.

Vladeck, B. C. (1980). *Unloving care: The nursing home tragedy.* New York: Basic Books.

Waldman, S. (1985). A legislative history of nursing home care. In Ronald J. Vogel & Hans E. Palmer (Eds.), *Long-term care: Perspectives from research and demonstrations.* Rockville, MD: Aspen.

Weir, R. F. & Gostin, L. (1990). Decisions to abate life-sustaining treatment for nonautonomous patients: Ethical standards and legal liability for physicians after *Cruzan*. *Journal of American Medical Association, 264*(14), 1846–1853.

Willcocks, D., Peace, S., & Kellaher, L. (1987). *Private lives in public places*. New York: Travistock Publications.

Study Questions

- Define "highest practicable" level of mental and physical health. How would you know it when you had it?
- How would you establish "thresholds" of acceptable care outcomes above which poor quality of care would be identified?
- How would a model of "continuing quality improvement" be incorporated into a nursing theory or process?
- What are the advantages and disadvantages of private insurance for institutional long-term care? For community-based long-term care (i.e., home care)?
- What should private insurance cover? Medications? Dentures? Prosthetics? Replacement costs if lost? Personal care at home? Instrumental ADL (i.e., shopping, banking, etc.)?
- What are the differences, if any, between process and outcome of institutional accreditation by government and private agencies?
- What kinds of input is it reasonable to expect from consumer groups with respect to quality imperatives for long-term care?

DATE DUE

GAYLORD			PRINTED IN U.S.A.